NATIONAL UNIVERSITY PUBLICATIONS

KENNIKAT PRESS CORP.

90 SOUTH BAYLES AVENUE
PORT WASHINGTON, N. Y. 11050 · (516) 883-0570

Book No. 9240

We take pleasure in sending you this review copy of

ON THE ENDINGS OF WARS

**Edited by Stuart Albert and
Edward C. Luck**

DATE OF PUBLICATION November 7, 1980

PRICE $17.50

*Direct quotation in reviews is limited to 500 words unless special
permission is given.*

Please send us two copies of your review

ON THE ENDINGS OF WARS

Kennikat Press
National University Publications
Series in Political Science

ON THE ENDINGS OF

WARS

Edited by
STUART ALBERT *and* **EDWARD C. LUCK**

National University Publications
KENNIKAT PRESS // 1980
Port Washington, N.Y. // London

Manufactured in the United States of America

Published by
Kennikat Press Corp.
Port Washington, N.Y. / London

Library of Congress Cataloging in Publication Data
Main entry under title:

On the endings of wars

    (Political science series) (National university publications)
    Bibliography: p.
    Includes index.
    1. War. I. Luck, Edward C. II. Albert, Stuart, 1941-
U21.2.E53   355.02'8   79-19238
ISBN 0-8046-9240-8

CONTENTS

SECTION III: CIVILIAN AND MILITARY PERCEPTIONS

SECTION IV: HONOR AND MORALITY

ON THE ENDINGS OF WARS

CONTRIBUTORS

Stuart Albert, visiting Associate Professor at the University of Illinois, is a social psychologist interested in the study of change and transitions throughout the life cycle. He has held positions at the University of Michigan, the Graduate Center of the City University of New York, and the University of Pennsylvania.

Berenice A. Carroll is Associate Professor of Political Science at the University of Illinois, Urbana-Champaign. She is the author of *Design for Total War: Arms and Economics in the Third Reich*, the editor of *Liberating Women's History: Theoretical and Critical Essays*, and the author of numerous articles and essays appearing in books and journals. From 1972 to 1980, she served as the editor of *Peace and Change: A Journal of Peace Research*. She has been active in various local and national branches of the peace movement and the women's movement.

J. Glenn Gray was a philosopher, teacher, writer and scholar. His publications include three books, *The Warriors: Philosophic Reflections on Men in Battle*, *The Promise of Wisdom*, and *Hegel's Hellenic Ideal*, as well as numerous contributions to philosophic anthologies and journals. He served as the editor for the most recent English translations of Martin Heidegger's works. Professor Gray taught at Colorado College from 1948 until his death in 1977.

Jay L. Kaplan is Assistant Vice President of the Criminal Justice Institute in New York City. He was formerly Assistant Professor of International Relations at the State University of New York at Geneseo. He has written numerous articles on both foreign and domestic policy issues.

Robert Jay Lifton is Foundations' Fund Research Professor of Psychiatry at Yale University School of Medicine. He has been involved for twenty-five years with studies of holocaust, war, and extreme situations. His book, *Death in Life: Survivors of Hiroshima*, won the National Book Award in 1969; and a study of Vietnam veterans, *Home From the War*, was nominated for the National Book Award in 1974. He has also been concerned with questions of theory, and in his new book, *The Broken Connection: On Death and the Continuity of Life*, he develops a new psychological paradigm that emerges from the full body of his work.

David Little is Professor of Religion at the University of Virginia. During 1979-1980, he was visiting Professor of Comparative Religious Ethics at Amherst College and during the Summer of 1980 was co-director of the NEH Seminar on Comparative Religious Ethics at Brown University. In 1978 he co-authored *Comparative Religious Ethics* with Sumner B. Twiss.

Edward C. Luck is Deputy to the Vice President for Research and Policy Studies of the United Nations Association of the USA (UNA-USA). From 1974 to 1977, he was Project Director for the UNA-USA National Policy Panel on Conventional Arms Control and was a Consultant of the RAND Corporation from 1973 to 1976. He has written numerous articles and given frequent Congressional testimonies in the fields of arms control, national security, and Soviet foreign and defense policy.

Adam Yarmolinsky is of Counsel to the firm of Kominers, Fort, Schlefer and Boyer in Washington, D.C. From 1977 to 1979, he was Counselor to the US Arms Control and Disarmament Agency. Previously he served as Ralph Waldo Emerson University Professor at the University of Massachusetts, Professor of Law at Harvard Law School, Principal Depty Assistant Secretary of Defense for International Security Affairs, and in several other legal, public affairs, editorial and government positions. He is the author of *Recognition of Excellence* (1960), *The Military Establishment* (1971) and numerous articles, and is the editor of *Case Studies in Personnel Security* (1955).

EDWARD C. LUCK and
STUART ALBERT

INTRODUCTION

Despite the thousands of scholarly volumes devoted to it, war remains something of an enigma. Perhaps the least understood, and certainly the least studied, aspect of wars is how they end.[1] The very destructiveness of modern warfare has led many analysts to focus on how wars begin and how they might best be prevented. Yet, whether by plan or accident, wars continue to occur, rarely following a course anticipated by any of the participants. It is conceivable that a better comprehension of the ending process would also contribute to our understanding of the causes of war. This book presents an interdisciplinary analysis of the national values, attitudes, and perceptions associated with the transition from war to peace.

Numerous historians have traced the rise and fall of civilizations through their success or failure on the battlefield. Likewise, military analysts have been chiefly concerned with how to prepare for, how to fight, and—implicitly—how to win wars. However, the traditional military yardstick presents an overly simplistic picture of war endings. Success on the battlefield cannot guarantee the postwar attainment of desired political or economic objectives. Besides, these goals may not be defined precisely before the war and are likely to shift during the course of the conflict. In an age of limited war, nations are not always fully committed to achieving a decisive military victory, preferring a less costly political compromise, particularly if a military stalemate appears likely. Wars between relatively small states are often settled through great power intervention or international conflict resolution efforts before they can be resolved militarily.

Thus, the study of war endings clearly should not be restricted to an analysis of military strategy and performance.

Domestic support for the war effort can be as important in determining the outcome as the military situation. Various domestic groups or members of an alliance may have very different conceptions concerning how to end the war and divide the spoils. Certainly, all participants will not share identical expectations regarding the nature of the postwar world. During much of the conflict, military goals and strategies may seem paramount, but political, social, psychological and moral considerations are likely to gain prominence as the end approaches. Public officials and national opinion leaders may feel compelled to present a program for war termination and postwar reconstruction which appears to justify the losses incurred during the fighting.

War endings are difficult to foresee, since they rarely meet the expectations of any of the participants. Aggressors tend to begin wars with optimism, not anticipating or planning for defeat. If given a reasonable alternative, few government leaders would choose to enter a war with little prospect of securing prewar objectives. For instance, U.S. nuclear strategy stresses deterrence rather than defense.

Even if the failure of the war effort is foreseen, national leaders may distort information concerning the course of the war in order to provide a more optimistic picture. This may serve legitimate functions such as building morale, avoiding defeatism, and discouraging collaboration with the enemy. Yet government leaders may hide the costs and probable failure of the war effort simply to lessen public criticism of their policies. The public may pressure for total victory as the only adequate justification for their wartime sacrifices. Government peace overtures during latter stages of the conflict may appeal to some portions of the public, but also may incite domestic charges of appeasement and weakness.

In general, public policy seems to be oriented more toward beginnings than endings. Domestic programs may begin with an influx of enthusiasm and funding which is withdrawn in the end. Recognizing this process, ambitious administrators may engage in "creaming," or moving on to other areas before a given program fails. The public does not always identify endings with beginnings, often failing to recognize the continuity of policies. Thus, near-term results may be more important to a policy maker's career than long-term implications.

As the Vietnam War demonstrated, the ending process often lacks order and coherence. The war may have multiple endings, ending at different times for different participants. While the military contest may have a finite ending, the political, social, and psychological issues may not be resolved even years after the formal end of hostilities. The disorderly nature of the ending process may create the strains on which future conflicts are based. Moreover, each war produces widely held lessons concerning how the next war should be avoided or fought, and these lessons are translated into military strategies and forces. In this way, the ending of one war may help shape the beginning of the next.

Professor Albert, in discussing the "Dynamics and Paradoxes of the Ending Process," analyzes how everyday social endings condition our perception of and response to the endings of international conflict. He notes that the inherently paradoxical nature of the ending process has complicated our comprehension of war endings, especially the gradual termination of the Vietnam War. According to Edward Luck, the American emphasis on deterrence theory since World War II has discouraged extensive public analysis of nuclear war endings, certainly a vital issue if deterrence should fail. He analyzes the arguments and assumptions of the early nuclear strategists and discusses their validity today.

War has been widely perceived as an epic test of national strength and will in which the stronger nation or coalition emerges triumphant over a vanquished foe. This traditional image is challenged in Section II. Professor Carroll cites numerous historical cases which bring into question the "mystique of dominance." Indeed, she argues that victory and defeat are symbiotic relationships and that the "fruits of victory" are largely dependent on the attitudes and actions of the defeated state. Professor Kaplan examines the difficulties faced by a victorious coalition in securing more than minimal postwar objectives. These problems are illustrated through a case study of post–World War I relations between the Allies and Germany.

In the third section, Professors Yarmolinsky and Lifton explore the divergent attitudes and expectancies of both combatants and noncombatants toward war endings, with particular reference to Vietnam. Professor Yarmolinsky focuses on the effect of differing civilian and military perspectives on the conduct and termination of limited wars. In discussing the experiences of the returning POWs from Vietnam, Professor Lifton analyzes the contending roles and images which the public expected the POWs to fulfill.

The final section considers issues of honor and morality which are often confronted honestly only after the termination of hostilities.

Professor Gray examines the philosophical concept of honor, both on the interpersonal and international levels, and provides historical examples of its application to war endings. Basing his analysis on "just war" criteria, Professor Little evaluates U.S. policy towards ending its direct involvement in the Vietnam War.

The editors gratefully acknowledge the support of the Center for Research in Cognition and Affect of the City University of New York in permitting the sections by Lifton, Gray, Carroll, and Albert to be used in this volume.

NOTES

1. Exceptions include Fred Charles Ikle, *Every War Must End* (New York: Columbia University Press, 1971); "How Wars End," *Annals of the American Academy of Political and Social Science,* November 1970, ed. William T. R. Fox; Paul Kecskemeti, *Strategic Surrender: The Politics of Victory and Defeat* (Stanford, California: Stanford University Press, 1958); Herman Kahn, William Pfaff, and Edmund Stillman, "War Termination, Issues and Concepts" (Harmon-on-Hudson, New York: Hudson Institute, June 1968); Herman Kahn, *On Escalation: Metaphors and Scenarios* (New York: Frederick A. Praeger, 1965); and Berenice A. Carroll, "How Wars End: An Analysis of Some Current Hypotheses," *Journal of Peace Research* 4 (1969), 295–320.

Section I

UNDERSTANDING ENDINGS

STUART ALBERT

1
DYNAMICS AND PARADOXES
OF THE ENDING PROCESS

As the Vietnam War recedes into history we continue to be faced with the task of making sense of it. It has become increasingly apparent that we not only lack the power to control events, but in many instances we lacked the categories to comprehend them. The focus in this chapter is on the ending of the Vietnam War. Repeatedly we have returned to World War II for a sense of what an ending should be like, for not only was World War II the central experience of a generation, but its ending brought a feeling of long-sought victory and of closure. The objective of this chapter is to examine the ways in which we interpret the ending of a war based on our daily experience with other kinds of endings. This chapter develops the thesis that our understanding of the way in which a war ends, and our expectancies about the way it should end, are derived from the experience of transition and separations in everyday life.

In the largest sense, the theme and study of endings runs counter to the grain of American thought. This is a country whose roots are found in beginnings, in open spaces, in the ideology of growth, in the appeal of the frontier, in westward expansion, and in the exploration of outer space. To situate the theme of endings we must recognize two models of change. The first is a model in which change is achieved by growth and expansion. The new social, economic, or political form is simply constructed with little regard for what already exists. Congruent with the ideology of the Old West, when new construction becomes difficult in one location, the entrepreneur simply moves on to uninhabited territory.

By contrast there is a second model for the introduction of new forms, a model of change by replacement. The principle articulated by this model is that to begin something new one must end or at least transform something old. It is the growing applicability of a model of change by replacement with its assumption of a finite universe that motivates the search for knowledge about the ending process, for so much of the American concern with endings has violence at its core. Although this may be an overstatement, the dominant way this country knows how to end anything is to declare war on it. We declare war on poverty, on cancer, and sometimes on the field of battle, on life itself. The root metaphor for the model of growth by expansion is birth, and the root metaphor for the model of change based on replacement is death. These two metaphors no doubt color the image of the two models and reinforce the tenacity with which we hold on to the former. We are nonetheless witnessing a shift from the model of change based on expansion to one based on replacement, so that the problem of designing satisfactory endings becomes one of the central problems of our time.

The objective of this chapter is to provide an analysis of the ending process in everyday life, to locate in these everyday endings the source of our expectancies about the way an ending process should be conducted— expectancies that I believe have guided our response to the ending of the Vietnam War, at times contributing a false sense of hope, but more likely, when they were disconfirmed, creating a sense of frustration and confusion. A variety of endings will be examined from a graduation ceremony to the ending structure of a sporting event. While the analysis presented here can only be suggestive, we seek in these diverse endings a sense of what people expect an ending to contain and how it should proceed.

This undertaking is, in a sense, a pioneering venture. There are a number of reasons why the endings of social and cultural events have been largely ignored as a site for systematic conceptual and empirical inquiry within psychology. First, the detailed structure of an ending is very difficult to observe. Endings are often high-speed events. One person will say to another, "Well, so long Bill, see you next week. Say hello to the wife, right? Bye, bye"—and before you know it, the process of separation has been completed. Second, the ending stage of human interaction appears to be almost completely constructed from insignificant cultural rituals. It seems to be dominated by stylized forms and therefore appears an unlikely site for the study of important human issues. But not only are endings events of high speed allegedly comprised of a mechanical sequence of cultural rituals, but an ending is also an event that occurs precisely at that time in the life of a communication system when the system is intentionally breaking itself apart. The working of a system that is dismantling itself is particularly difficult to observe in detail, for the acquisition of knowledge about social events is made immeasurably easier when these events have permanence and stability.

The problem of endings has not been studied for another reason, and that is that everyday endings are often believed to be simple events, so that the scientific yield from their detailed study would be minimal. There is, in fact, a sense in which many endings are simple and uncomplicated phenomena, but much of the apparent simplicity is simply a result of our failure to record the fine-grained detail of the event—first because we are often blind to the complexity of those actions that are accomplished with ease, and second, to pay attention to our behavior in the midst of performing it so as to discover its complexity might well limit our ability to perform that behavior in the first place. At a minimum it would jeopardize its spontaneity. It is almost as if, by analogy, we began to think about our breathing, only to find ourselves short of breath as a result. Much of the real and apparent simplicity of everyday endings is complexly achieved.

At the interpersonal level, we can formulate the problem of endings as the problem of describing the processes by which a pair of individuals are together at time 1 and are separated at time 2.

Let us approach the problem of endings by examining one of its solutions. Consider a boxing match. A boxing match, as we all know, consists of rounds, that is, lengths of time specified in advance. Consider the situation if the concept of a round is eliminated and the boxers in the midst of the match are to decide when and if they should take a break. Let them further decide when to sleep and rest and when to begin the fight again. Let the fighters together with the spectators decide when the fight is over, and let them at this point debate who won and who lost. Unstructure a prizefight in this way, dismantle its largely temporal structure that solves the problem of ending in advance, and who among us would be brave enough to buy a ticket to the match, particularly if we gave the fighters something more lethal than their fists and let them decide the exact terrain over which the fight would take place.

In this instance, the problem of when an ending will take place has been solved before the fight begins. Usually this kind of agreed-upon temporal agenda to which the participants are bound does not exist. It is therefore necessary to examine how a sense of closure is achieved by examining some of the events that typically occur during the terminal phase of social interaction. One such event is the presence of a summary. For example, "Well Bill, I'm glad we had a chance to talk about X and Y." Let us examine some of the reasons why a summary may work both to reflect and precipitate an ending, what criteria we expect a *successful* summary to have, and some of the dilemmas that result when these criteria are in conflict.

It is easy to think of examples of summaries. For example, "It was nice seeing you again." "Well, that about covers it." When a person retires there is often a party to which all persons who are important in that person's life come. Someone usually makes a speech, and the party and that speech are likely to contain summaries. A war memorial is, in a sense, a symbolic summary of an event, stating the occasion and the participants.

One of the defining characteristics of a summary is that it is selective— that is, when we summarize something, we do not repeat the entire encounter. Agreement by the participants that a summary of their encounter be selective establishes the principle that not everything in the encounter is worth saying over or needs to be said over. But this questions the continued existence of the encounter, for it is the requirement that something needs to be said rather than merely thought about privately that is the basis for the interaction. An agreement on what need not be said is the first step towards agreement that nothing need be said. Thus, any time a summary is present, for whatever reason, one result is the implication that the encounter need not be continued. Indeed, under certain conditions summary statements may be advanced in order to make use of this implication so that their presence both reflects an ending already in progress and, at the same time, helps bring it about.

Summaries occur during endings for another reason. By bringing together many diverse aspects from the long history of the encounter and displaying them for observation at one time, a summary allows the participants to make certain other kinds of judgments often associated with and sometimes even required by the ending process. For example, has each individual been treated fairly? If one individual feels disadvantaged he may wish the encounter to continue, in hope of restoring his losses. Only when all the relevant evidence is assembled can such a judgment be made, for ethical and moral judgments usually demand a complete presentation of the evidence. Ethical judgments are extremely difficult to make when the critical pieces of information on which they will be based lie scattered and buried throughout the history of the encounter. Thus, summary statements may be present during the ending of social interaction because such statements serve the function of unearthing information necessary to determine whether equity and justice has been achieved.

However, if a summary is too selective and omits something of importance, it will fail as an ending device. A businessman, for example, who has discussed a variety of financial matters with his partner will not allow his partner to end the conversation by saying, "Well, we talked about A and B today," if in fact the conversation also included C. He will reply, "What about C?" unless it is somehow clear that C was implied in the summary.

One of the most interesting difficulties of constructing an adequate summary derives from the impossibility of simultaneously satisfying certain criteria of successful summaries. One such dilemma is between the need for a complete—that is, relatively unselective—summary, and the need to create the illusion of equity and justice. Particularly in a complex hostile encounter, equity or justice is usually achieved by a process in which each individual ignores some portion of the injury done to the other. Since there is no universally accepted moral calculus for weighing and balancing each and every injury, equity is achieved by approximation. On the one hand the more complete and comprehensive a summary is, the more it is likely to succeed as an ending device; but on the other hand, the more complete the summary, the more likely it is that instances of unresolved inequity will be discovered. At a minimum there will be more instances of injury and harm that will have to be weighed and balanced against each other.

The resolution of the dilemma between the need for a complete and yet equitable summary is sometimes sought in the device of a distorted summary. The participants may attempt to manage the news about what is happening. A true statement of the encounter may be sacrificed in order to bring it to an end. The use of a distorted summary is made more difficult by the presence of third parties whose observation of the encounter leads to a reconstruction of its history at variance with the distortions introduced by the participants for the purpose of constructing a summary that will be useful in achieving an ending. There are, of course, limits to the degree to which a summary can be distorted, for if it is to be effective the summary must not only be selective and somehow complete, but it must also be regarded as true.

If the construction of an adequate summary is this difficult, perhaps it can be omitted from the ending process entirely. But some of the functions of a summary are not easily replaceable. For example, a summary forecasts the possibility of redundancy. A summary repeats information from the past and hence contains the implication that there may be little new to add, and if there is nothing to add, there is no reason to continue the encounter.

Furthermore, a summary brings information together in such a way as to make its storage and retrieval easier. If we do not believe that an event or encounter will be remembered, it is unlikely that we will allow it to come to an end. This is probably true even if the event is somewhat unpleasant, for we probably act on the fear expressed by Santayana that if we cannot remember the past we are condemned to repeat it.

In addition to creating a distorted summary, another attempted solution to the problem of constructing a summary for an inequitable encounter is the device of a dual summary, that is, a superficial public summary to which all parties can agree, having negotiated the proper degree of selectivity and comprehensiveness, together with a private summary intended for a select few which allows each individual to provide his or her own interpretation of events. The device of a dual summary will always raise the issue of secrecy, for to be effective, the private summary must not become public.

What can we say about the attempt to formulate summary statements for the Vietnam War? What seems apparent in retrospect is that most if not all of the attempted justifications for bringing the war to an end also contained an explicit or implicit summary of what the war was about. The need to obtain a complete summary of the war and the alleged dangers of doing so was the central issue surrounding the publication of the Pentagon Papers. But the more a summary of U.S. involvement in Vietnam revealed a series of mistakes, miscalculations, unethical acts, etc., the more such evidence could be used to justify continued presence in order to remedy the situation at the same time that it provided the motivation for leaving. Thus, it is no surprise that there was a large battle over information, its truth, and its completeness.

The same issue of trying to find out what was going on in order to bring it to an end was also raised in Watergate, and one could argue that part of our fascination with Watergate was that it dealt with many of the same issues as the war in Vietnam, but on home ground with an American cast. It therefore made the feelings and emotions of the war intelligible: issues like what activities are justifiable to preserve the party in power, how is the opposition party to be treated, what is the national interest, etc.

Traditionally, the end of a war is most dramatically summarized in a parade. A parade is a string of symbols standing for the event the parade represents. A military parade, which typically ends a war, includes all branches of the armed services together with a variety of weapons. Usually the parade takes place in what has been designated as the center of town, in the heart of the people. Spectators of all kinds and of all ages come to watch. The people in the parade carry something we call a flag, a symbol of their collective identity.

In contrast to World War II, there was no parade of any consequence at the end of the Vietnam War, not only because the war did not end in victory, but also because the dilemma of completeness versus the discovery of even greater inequity and contradiction could not be solved for this parade. What would a parade as a complete summary of the war have consisted of? At a minimum it would mean flower children alongside tanks, guerrilla theater next to smart bombs, Norman Mailer marching at the head of the Veterans of Foreign Wars. It would have meant children and napalm side by side. The course of this Vietnam War could not be subsumed under solely military considerations, and so a military parade as a summary ending was impossible. A parade at the conclusion of the Vietnam War would have had to include elements so diverse and mutually antagonistic that their juxtaposition would have symbolized the deep fissures of dissent about the war, its justification, and its meaning; the nation was perhaps justifiably unprepared for such a spectacle in the absence of an integrative or healing context.

To summarize the issue of summaries. We have come to expect that endings contain summaries and that these summaries be selective yet complete, that they deal with the issue of omission, that they negotiate the dilemma between the canons of truth and the requirements of distortion. These expectancies are developed from the thousands of routine social events that we accomplish with relative ease in everyday life and whose collective achievement forms our social world. In fact, part of our optimism is based on the fact that such very subtle and complex problems are solved with such apparent ease.

Let us consider another observable feature of many endings, namely an attempt at what might be called individualization, a process by which each individual in an encounter reaffirms that his individual identity is distinct from the social encounter that is ending.

As William James and Charles Horton Cooley pointed out at the turn of the century, a person comes to know who he is by the way other people respond to him. A person has, in Cooley's phrase, "a looking glass self," a self constructed according to its reflection in the mirrors held by others around it. An ending entails the termination or momentary suspension of those aspects of self-identity that were defined in relation to others, and therefore may pose a threat to the identity of an individual whose self was somehow bound up in the relationship with the other person (for example, a trusting person must have someone to trust). To emerge from a social encounter it is therefore often necessary to present evidence of a distinct individual identity apart from that provided by the social encounter. A parade, with its string of national symbols and its feeling of patriotism symbolizes the continued strength of a nation following the conclusion of a conflict in which the nation's identity and continued existence was itself at stake. (Watergate was, if only in part, a reflection of a nation's attempt to redefine and reaffirm its positive identity at the conclusion of a conflict that threatened it.)

When Walter Cronkite says, "This is Walter Cronkite, CBS News," as part of the ending of his broadcast, he does so not only for our benefit, so we know whom we have been listening to, but also out of a habit whose functional origin is the need to affirm an individual identity at the point of separation. Similarly, it is no accident that we sign our letters at the bottom, not simply to indicate that we have written all that went before, but also to indicate that it is "I" who is doing the writing.

The return of the prisoners of war at the end of the Vietnam War was a restorative act of a body whose members had been held captive. Our collective investment in their return is part of the process of individuation that we have come to expect in all endings in which the unit which is ending affirms its wholeness and identity at the time of ending. We suggest that Watergate raised the indignation of the nation, not simply because the most damning facts were well hidden, but also because as part of the ending of the Vietnam War the country felt a need to believe in the integrity of its government, that unit which was symbolically extricating itself from a war. That an attack upon the presidency was ultimately possible was testimony to the fact that an ending to the war had largely been accomplished.

Our analysis thus far has focused on the summary and the process of individuation as potential sources of our expectancies regarding the ending process. Both of these processes rely heavily on the existence of a reliable symbol system. Let us now turn to a process which deemphasizes the role of linguistic and symbolic processes and focuses on man's limitations as a biological organism.

One common process of ending is one in which the organism consumes the resources which sustain the encounter. For example, one person may say to another, "I'm tired and want to go to bed." The participant indicates that there is a personal resource which is being used up faster than it can be replenished. Extremes of emotional response, both love and hate, may be similarly successful in depleting the emotional resources of the participants. The implication is that an encounter can be ended more quickly if the rate at which the resource is being used up can be accelerated. The parallel implication for the ending of a hostile encounter is that we may expect a period of intensification prior to ending. Ending an encounter by increasing the rate at which critical resources are expended is rooted in our biology, but it is also directly relevant to the concepts of waste and efficiency. Thus, whatever the resources that sustain an encounter, our claim is that we must often provide evidence that they have been used up in order to end, even if the resources are bombs.

If the summary process conceptualized the past history of the social encounter, the continuity process to which we now turn deals largely with the future. The process of asserting a continuity of relationship is one of the most important and complex of the various termination processes that we will consider. A simple example is when one person says, "See you tomorrow," which implies that a relationship continues even if the encounter does not. The word for good-bye in many languages has a strong continuity connotation: "Auf Wiedersehn" (until I see you again), "Ate Logo" (until I see you again soon). The continuity principle denies that the essential meaning of the encounter is one that requires a physical co-presence of the interaction. It asserts a paradox. To end, it is necessary to affirm a nonending; continuity can be established by a promise, a pledge, an oath, a contract, or a treaty.

Frequently we hear as part of the ending of a social encounter the expression of good wishes: "Have a safe trip." "Take care." Part of the function of these statements is one of continuity, namely, the wish that the departing individual remain unharmed so that he be able to return and take up the interaction where it left off.

The obvious example of the need for continuity on the international level is the establishment of closer ties between the United States and China.

Nixon's trip to China served to establish an overreaching relationship with a region of the world in such a way that he could begin to end the Vietnam conflict by reference to the larger geopolitical issues of which Vietnam was only one part. One ends a war in Vietnam by establishing an enduring relationship with Asia.

The need to believe in the ill-fated policy of Vietnamization lay in the depth of the need for continuity, the negation of which is abandonment. We would be able to leave Vietnam because the Vietnamese would be able to fight on as if we were there. The interpersonal origin of the concept of Vietnamization is the need for intergenerational continuity. When will the child be sufficiently strong and independent as a result of the right up-bringing to carry on the family name alone? In Vietnam one withdrew troops but later promised foreign aid. In terms of our expectancies, we suggest that the joint affirmation of ending and nonending is as necessary as it is confusing.

Let us now turn our attention to another characteristic feature of everyday ending. This is a process of redefinition by which the purpose of an encounter becomes redefined not as an end in itself but as a means for accomplishing some future end. A common illustration is provided by the graduation speaker who perennially asks the departing graduates to believe that their education is a means for achieving some future goal. Presumably the day-to-day activities of school had a meaning and justification of their own, but for the speaker to remind the student that his activities were a means to an end is not so much to reduce the importance of those activities (although it does do that), but to relocate the value for those activities in some future time. To remove the justification for the existence of an event from the event itself and shift it to the future requires a belief in the future. This belief is particularly difficult to hold in a time of violence when the idea of a future itself is in question. Nonetheless, our claim is that the shift of justification from present to future creates a boundary between the two that facilitates an ending.

To help the graduating student move into the future, all that is of possible use for him, such as a summary of his educational experience, is given to him as a psychological and practical gift as he leaves. Of course, the summary provided by the graduation speaker and by the event itself is magically incomplete, for the claim is made that the individual will discover unknown uses for his education. He is told that he knows things he does not know he knows, and moreover, that these things will be important to him.

Applying a similar logic, we were told as part of the attempt to end the Vietnam War that the war was not an end in itself, but rather a means to a future world of peace and justice, and the logic here is just as slippery. We know that to justify the present on the basis of an uncertain future which contains its rewards requires an extraordinary leap of faith. Nonetheless, we are all accustomed to this subtle sleight of hand because it is endemic to the commonplace endings of our culture.

Figure 1.1

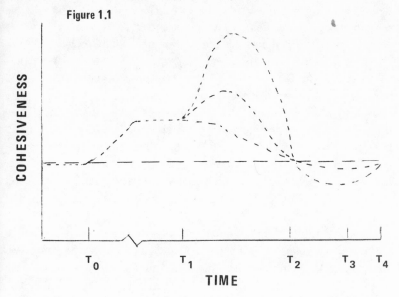

In order to examine several other characteristics of the ending process, it is useful to be able to plot the attraction between two individuals as a function of time. Figure 1.1 represents some hypothetical paths that attraction may take. Let us assume that persons A and B have some average level of attraction. At point T_0 they meet and engage in the rituals of greeting. This is indicated by an increase in the expression of attraction and cohesiveness at that time. During the actual duration of the encounter, attraction may vary. At time T_1, we approach the beginning of the end. Let us consider several alternative paths. One is based on the assumption that an ending occurs simply through the weakening of social bonds, a steady process of detachment. This would mean that an outside observer would detect a progressive reduction in mutual attraction during the terminal phase of the encounter illustrated by the lower dotted lines in the figure. The ending simply peters out, but we believe that this is a relatively atypical occurrence. Let us consider a second path that we believe is more common and one that illustrates the paradox of an increase in observed attraction prior to ending. Two individuals nearing the end of an encounter will often express pleasure in having met and perhaps even hug or kiss. The intensity of positive feeling that is expressed at the end of a social encounter will often be greater than at any other time during the encounter with perhaps the exception of the greeting (assuming of course that the encounter is not a hostile one, although even then the desire to end on a positive note is present). We illustrate this increase in the expression of attraction by a rise in the curve.

For now, let us just consider this portion of the curve only up to time T_2, and, without raising the question of when an ending is characterized by an increase in liking and attraction, let us consider some of the reasons why such an increase might occur.

At first glance, the summary process would appear to be one of the primary mechanisms for producing a rise in attraction prior to ending. It is a mechanism for placing the positive affects that are distributed throughout the encounter together at one place. But there is nothing inherent in the summary process that requires that it summarize only instances of positive feeling. Thus, a summary may be necessary, but it is clearly not sufficient.

The continuity principle provides part of the answer, for if individuals are to express some desire for continuing a relationship, there must be some justification for a future meeting. And this justification is often found in the pleasantness of the present encounter. Thus, we envision a two-stage process. A summary brings together the positive features of the social encounter so that continuity can be asserted, and we suggest that this is the order in which the two processes usually occur. "Well, I certainly enjoyed that," followed by, "We'll have to do it again." Since the summary deals with the past and the continuity with the future, it is also fitting to have this order, since it corresponds to the anistrophy of time.

Let us briefly mention several other reasons for a possible increase in attraction prior to ending. Perhaps the most obvious explanation is that attraction is a response to the fear of being isolated or of being alone. Or perhaps, as Irving Goffman has suggested, there are prohibitions against the expression of intimacy during an encounter, which may be safely lifted only with the knowledge that the encounter is about to end. It is also possible that individuals dramatize—hence increase—their feelings of liking and attraction so as to better retain them in memory, and a memory of the encounter would allow them to take the encounter with them symbolically.

Applying this analysis to the ending of the Vietnam War suggests that it is not surprising that as we sought to withdraw from Vietnam we simultaneously felt a need to express heightened support for the Vietnam regime. Our claim is that the reasons for such support are rooted in the expectancies we develop about endings based on our experience of hundreds and thousands of "ordinary and unremarkable" endings in everyday life. We have come to expect an ending of a social encounter to be more positive than any other portion. The reasons for this increase in attraction are not simply the result of arbitrary rituals, but reflect very fundamental processes by which individuals separate the past from the future and deal with feelings of isolation and abandonment.

Let us now examine that portion of the figure to the right of time T_2 which indicates that after an ending, there may be a period when attraction is even lower than when the encounter began. We refer to this period as a refractory period after the biological phenomenon, a period of time after a nerve cell fires during which it is not possible for that cell to fire again. Let us give an example of a refractory period at the social level.

Imagine a large farewell party for an individual who is about to leave on a European trip. All of his friends arrive at the party. Gifts are given to the departing individual. The mood is pleasant. After a prolonged farewell, he leaves. He drives to the airport, but for some inexplicable reason changes his mind and drives back to the party. He presents himself at the hostess's home, where the party is still going on. He announces that he decided not to go. What happens next isn't too pleasant. The more people who came to that farewell party, the more expensive the gifts, the more lavish the food and beverage, the more prolonged the speeches, the more intense the emotional outpouring, the greater the problem when that departed individual returns from the airport.

Consider a second example related to me by one of my students. A friend of this student discovered that one of her acquaintances had passed away. She was shocked. She sat down and wrote a letter of condolence to this person's parents, but for some reason did not mail the letter. Several weeks later she discovered that the report of her friend's death was a case of mistaken identity. Her friend in fact was alive. But because she had gone through the process of ending a relationship, she could not bring herself to interact with her friend for several weeks. Having ended a relationship, she found herself unable to begin again.

The concept of a refractory period, and more precisely, our expectancy that such a period of time exists, can be related at the international level to the concept of isolationism and to the fear that ending a relationship too completely makes restarting it, even when it is in both parties' interest to do so, a very difficult task. The United States may be unwilling or perhaps psychologically unable to recommit its forces even if necessary, if in some sense, the war is believed to have ended. A dilemma arises from the fact that those factors which produce a faster ending, a more complete ending, a more irreversible ending, are precisely those which also create a refractory period, and it is the refractory period, with its connotations of impotence, that is greatly feared. A successful ending, therefore, is one that is accomplished with the necessary speed, but which at the same time, minimizes the length and depth of the subsequent refractory period. But that is not a simple task, for even if we carry out our analysis at the level of a farewell party, how shall we eliminate the difficulty that results when the person returns from the airport, and still have a farewell party of the scale and magnitude required by the occasion?

Finally, let us turn to another concept derived from the study of human communication that appears to be a source of important expectancies. This is the concept of a pause, or as we prefer to describe it, the concept of a temporal hole or gap. (We prefer the notion of the gap because it carries no implications as to the meaning of this empty time period, the way a pause does.)

The nature of human communication is that we speak and write in discrete units. One word does not run into the next, nor one sentence indistinguishably into another. Rather, there are spaces and markers between these units. In our spoken discourse we have gaps or breaks if only because it is necessary to have periodic stops in order to breathe.

Under certain conditions, a temporal gap is considered a pause. Under certain conditions, a pause becomes embarrassing. That a temporal hole or gap occurs at exactly this point, is of this length, is filled with these activities and not others, is what defines it as a pause or rest period. In terms of our calendar, such a rest period may be a day of rest such as the Sabbath. Sometimes a temporal hole may be considered an interruption of an ongoing activity if there is reason to believe that the activity is not over.

In short, sometimes a temporal hole or gap will be a pause, will be an interruption, will be an ending, a moratorium, a cease-fire, or a New Year's Day truce. The concept of pause therefore punctuates not only our language but also social occasions and international events.

A long pause in a conversation often signals the end of the conversation as well as produces it. It is a space which both parties intentionally leave open under the provision that if no one fills it, it is because neither has anything to add. If a pause becomes wide enough it becomes an ending. A long pause becomes an ending and produces an ending because to continue an encounter with a long pause in it can become embarrassing, and what we mean by embarrassing is that a threat has been raised to the nature of the encounter.

We know that a pause can be a time of reflection, a time when previous events are considered, but we know also that inactivity during a temporal gap is restricted to certain specific conditions. Two lovers may remain in each other's presence but not speak primarily because they have that special kind of relationship called love. Usually we expect physical copresence without verbal dialogue to occur only under conditions of intimacy; otherwise, the pause is threatening or embarrassing. Therefore, we will not undertake a pause until we have some assurances of a special kind of relationship.

The fact that pauses are so often used as rest periods naturally leads us to expect that a cease-fire will be used for resupply and the strengthening of military fortifications. To use a pause for this purpose is as American as a pause that refreshes. Our outrage at violations of a cease-fire is undercut in part because we have come to expect such violations to occur, and the source of this expectancy is located in the frequency with which a pause is assumed to be a rest period rather than an ending.

In laying out our analysis of international actions against a background of cultural assumptions and implicit social rules we have implicitly developed an alternative language of explanation. We have developed the nuances of social action as forces which guide our perception and understanding of events.

Our point is simply this. We cannot take at face value the reasons given for a policy decision. The supposedly strategic game theoretical reason is actually a summary of a very complex set of arguments, many of them implicit, and hence of particular power.

For example, Nixon did not engage in terror bombing because he rationally decided to teach the North Vietnamese a lesson. If this indeed is what he though he was doing, then we ought to ask why he thought so, since they obviously did not think themselves the students of Nixon, nor did they think of their homeland as a classroom; and it is certainly true that to be a teacher one must have pupils. Rather, we may conclude that this is an interpretation that Nixon wanted the other side to accept. Yet he must have known that the North Vietnamese were very unwilling pupils. Our job is to make some of these cultural expectancies which guide these arguments more explicit. A reason for a particular policy decision is often shaped by the set of cultural expectancies within which it is embedded. The disembodiment of rational discourse from the rest of the human being is the most irrational of all acts.

We have sought to provide some understanding of the ending process by focusing on various paradoxes: that to end, one must affirm a non-ending; that an end often produces an expression of attraction greater than that expressed during any other point in the encounter; that to seek a complete account of what happened as a procedure for ending is to discover additional reasons for continuing.

If an ending is that kind of event that works, not in spite of the existence of paradoxes, but by means of them, then it is precisely that kind of event which, to be understood, requires particularly comprehensive and exhaustive knowledge; otherwise it is easy to believe that the contradictions one observes are simply irrational acts. (This is not to deny that sometimes they are irrational.)

Lacking very detailed knowledge of the ending process we will be totally unable to negotiate the horns of the various dilemmas hidden there. Rather than be impaled on the horns of one of these dilemmas, we have abdicated our authority for action to those who claimed to possess the required facts, and in doing so, have assumed that the possession of information was also the possession of knowledge. To recover the complexity of everyday endings and to provide a fine-grained analysis of the origin of our expectancies is to recover some of the authority for our actions.

What we need is an archaeology of human endings constructed according to culture, and sensitive to the dimensions of time, place, relationship, and situations, so as to uncover the structure of human endings and to grasp the origin of our feelings about them.

EDWARD C. LUCK

2

DETERRENCE THEORY AND NUCLEAR WAR ENDINGS

During the past three decades, many thoughtful volumes have been devoted to nuclear weapons and their effect on national security and military planning. Understandably, much of this interest has been directed towards how nuclear conflicts might begin and how they might best be avoided. Yet the question of how a nuclear war might end has rarely been considered.[1] Indeed, this remains one of the more "unthinkable" aspects of nuclear war.

Many analysts implicitly assume that a nuclear conflict would necessarily result in the total destruction of civilization as we know it in all of the participating countries and probably in most of the neutrals. Thus, there would be no winners: everyone would lose. Accordingly, the only meaningful mission for nuclear weapons is to deter war, rather than to win war.[2] They have failed their primary purpose if they must be employed in combat.

As will be seen below, these conclusions have been widely accepted in the United States since the dawn of the atomic age in 1945. The continued emphasis on nuclear deterrence during the past thirty years has largely precluded serious public analysis of nuclear war endings. This essay should not be interpreted as a critique of deterrence theory. Indeed, in the author's view, the primary role for both tactical and strategic nuclear weapons should be deterrence, not defense. There is no reason to believe that nuclear conflicts could be easily controlled or that "selective" strategic nuclear strikes should be considered an acceptable means of compensating for conventional setbacks. The very certainty that unacceptable and perhaps incomprehensible losses would result from a nuclear war has dissuaded most defense analysts from studying the ending process. If the ending is both inevitable and terrible, then the focus of analysis should quite properly be on preventing the outbreak of nuclear war. However, should deterrence fail, then policy-makers ought to have some understanding of how best to limit the damage and terminate the conflict. Since the mid-1950's, there has been considerable analysis of limited conventional and nuclear warfare, but much of the discussion has focused on strategies for fighting, rather than terminating, such a war.[3]

On the other hand, to analyze the possible endings of a future nuclear conflict may suggest that some endings are preferable to others and that some values may possibly be salvaged from the ashes of a nuclear exchange. In the eyes of some, such hypothesizing could undermine the emphasis on deterring rather than fighting a nuclear war—widely viewed as the keystone to military stability in a nuclear world. In particular, it is argued that the distinction in the public eye between conventional and strategic weapons must be strengthened.

Unilateral programs to develop, procure and deploy additional defensive or war-fighting capabilities could conceivably accelerate the strategic arms race along dangerous new paths. Defensive systems, such as ABMs and massive civil defense projects, can destabilize the strategic balance of terror by compromising the effectiveness of the adversary's second strike forces, thus weakening mutual deterrence. Moreover, the mission of defense generally requires a larger and more expensive strategic force posture than does simple deterrence, hence involving basic strategic policy issues in the complex politics of determining defense budgets.

Deterrence theory was first clearly enunciated in the mid-1950's and became the central core of official U.S. strategic doctrine during Secretary of Defense McNamara's tenure in the early 1960's. McNamara's flirtation with city-avoidance strategies, Secretary of Defense Schlesinger's advocacy of "selective first strikes" and the continuing ambiguities surrounding the possible first use of U. S. tactical nuclear weapons in Europe and Korea have all envisaged the possibility of employing nuclear weapons in a limited nuclear conflict. However, each of these strategies has been widely criticized and could be considered an aberration from the general emphasis on deterrence. Actually, each of these strategies has acknowledged deterrence as the primary role of nuclear weapons. Yet several of the essential assumptions underlying deterrence were dominant themes in numerous publications by both U.S. government and private analysts during the immediate post-World War II years of 1946–1948. Indeed, these often tacit assumptions appear to have been derived largely from the military lessons and popular impressions of strategic bombing campaigns during the war, combined with general awe of the atomic bomb's destructive power.

During World War II, strategic bombing performed primarily a war-fighting rather than deterrence function. Allied air superiority throughout the final years of the war permitted a generally one-sided application of strategic air power, which encouraged the acceptance of strategic bombing as an integral factor in winning a major conventional war. Although, as we shall see, the advent of nuclear weapons brought into question the meaning of "victory" in total war, the perceived importance of strategic bombing as a deterrent increased. Thus, strategic bombing remained a primary mission of the U.S. Air Force despite the dramatic advances in the technology of destruction.

Four closely related assumptions account for the early and continuing stress on deterrence rather than defense:

1. No single nation can for long monopolize the possession of atomic weapons, and, in a world of more than one nuclear power, a meaningful defense against a concerted nuclear attack is infeasible.

2. Nuclear weapons would be the decisive factor in any total war of the future, which is likely to begin with a massive surprise nuclear attack.

3. Cities and industrial facilities, not military installations, are likely to be the primary targets of strategic nuclear strikes.

4. The unavoidable widespread destruction on all sides from a nuclear conflict means that there can be no victor in such a war.

Therefore, if a nation is unwilling to accept either surrender or mutual suicide, then the only alternatives are international control of atomic weapons and/or deterrence of an opponent's first strike through the threat of terrible retaliation. Since the early efforts at international control failed completely, deterrence was widely viewed as the only rational means of avoiding nuclear devastation.

The terrifying conclusion that there existed no satisfactory defense against atomic bombardment was confirmed publicly only ten weeks after the destruction of Hiroshima and Nagasaki. In a Joint Declaration on Atomic Energy issued on November 15, 1945, President Truman, Prime Minister Attlee of Great Britain and Prime Minister King of Canada recognized that "the application of recent scientific discoveries to the methods and practice of war has placed at the disposal of mankind means of destruction hitherto unknown, against which there can be no adequate military defense, and in the employment of which no single nation can in fact have a monopoly."[4]

This pessimism was reflected in the writings of numerous civilian analysts during the next year. Active defense appeared to be impossible technologically, while national passive defense programs would have been extremely costly and socially disruptive. Two prominent physicists, Ivan A. Getting of M. I. T. and Henry Smyth of Princeton, concluded in December 1945 that there was no adequate active defense against atomic weapons.[5] "American security is endangered as never before," warned Caryl P. Haskins, "traditional modes of national defense are clearly inadequate." Harrison Brown, an atomic scientist, agreed that "the outlook for defending ourselves against an atomic bomb attack in a war of the future is a gloomy one. Any defense will, at best, be inadequate." Bernard Brodie, one of the earliest and most prominent civilian defense analysts, argued not only that no adequate defense existed, but that "the possibilities of its existence in the future are exceedingly remote."[6]

Invoking the prestige of the scientific community, Winfield W. Riefler pointed out that "In contrast to normal divergencies in viewpoint, the scientists who developed the bomb have been as one . . . in their warning that there is no defense against its destructive power except in widespread decentralization or deep underground shelter."[7] The Emergency Committee of Atomic Scientists, chaired by Albert Einstein, issued a list of propositions, supposedly "accepted by all scientists," including that "there is no military defense against atomic bombs, and none is to be expected."[8]

Several U.S. government reports shared this general sense of hopelessness regarding the possibility of developing an effective defense. The Secretary of State's Committee on Atomic Energy noted that "neither countermeasures nor the maintenance of secrecy about our own developments offers any adequate prospect of defense."[9] According to Joseph and Stewart Alsop, an unpublished U.S. Army General Staff study "discarded the hope . . . that a new miracle of science would provide a complete defense against atomic attack."[10] After assessing the potential damage to American cities from an atomic attack, the U.S. Strategic Bombing Survey concluded that "no defensive measures alone can long protect us. . . . Against full and sustained attacks they would be ineffectual palliatives."[11]

In theory, the problem of intercepting and destroying incoming bombers carrying nuclear weapons would be neither simpler nor more difficult than it would be for conventional bombers. However, as Hiroshima and Nagasaki so graphically demonstrated, the consequences of failure had increased drastically. As Harrison Brown phrased it, "The bomb that fell on Hiroshima closed the door to an age. One plane, one bomb, one city. A hundred bombs, a hundred cities."[12] In order to bring the point home to her readers, Francis Vivian Drake vividly warned that "it is now in the power of the atom-smashers to blot out New York with a single bomb. . . . Such a bomb can burn up in an instant every creature, can fuse steel buildings and smash the concrete into flying shrapnel."[13] Even before the bomb was completed, its potential destructive power against urban targets was recognized by U.S. policy-makers. In a memorandum to the President of April 25, 1945, Secretary of War Stimson predicted that the atomic bomb would be "the most terrible weapon ever known in human history, one bomb of which could destroy a whole city."[14]

Thus, a defense of cities against atomic weapons would need to be almost perfect, and, as numerous authors pointed out, a completely effective defense was far from possible. The Allies' recent experience in widespread strategic bombing campaigns reinforced this belief, suggesting that interception of attacking aircraft would be difficult even with local air superiority. In a lengthy analysis of the technical possibilities for defense, Ansley J. Coale evaluated the prospects for intercepting at least 90 percent of the attacking vehicles and concluded that the past record was discouraging. Moreover, he noted that even at this high rate, X00 bombs would be delivered to their targets if X,000 were launched in an attack, and the resulting damage would be disastrous.[15]

Several authors perceived an interaction throughout history between offensive and defensive weapons development, with a defense invented to counteract every offensive advancement. But, as the British military historian B. H. Liddell Hart pointed out:

While an antidote has been found for every new offensive development hitherto, there has always been a time-lag between such a development and the production of the antidote. The time-lag inevitably favours aggression. . . . As offensive developments become more powerful even a short time-lag becomes more dangerous. It is conceivable that an antidote may be found to the atomic bomb . . . but it is hard to see how such an antidote could be brought into operation until after hostilities actually began.[16]

Harrison Brown stressed that "in the war of the future, there can be no lag between offense and defense if catastrophe is to be avoided."[17] Moreover, as several authors noted, the immense destructive power of each atomic bomb required that the defense be fully effective at the very outset of hostilities—a most unlikely prospect.

According to Bernard Brodie, "one of the most frightening things about the bomb is that it makes the destruction of enemy cities an immeasurably cheaper process than it was before, cheaper not alone in terms of missiles but also in terms of the air forces necessary to do the job."[18] In an early comparison of the relative costs and effectiveness of defensive and offensive strategic capabilities, Dr. Brown concluded that "Atomic bombs make it possible for an offensive war to be waged very inexpensively. . . . Unfortunately, the expenses involved in a sudden offensive atomic war are small compared to the expenses involved in any attempt to establish a defense."[19] In other words, any increase in defensive forces can be offset more cheaply by additions to the adversary's offensive forces. Years later, this relationship was to become a prime argument against the series of proposed U.S. ABM systems.[20]

The task of defense was seriously complicated not only because of the increased destructiveness, but also because of the potential developments in means of delivery, namely rockets. Although the German V-1 and V-2 rockets did not prove to be decisive weapons during World War II, they pointed towards the development of more effective missiles in the future. It was widely noted that no V-2s were successfully intercepted.[21]

Furthermore, numerous authors recognized that the traditional American invulnerability from direct attack, which had been guaranteed by the surrounding oceans and friendly neighbors, would be eroded as the range of offensive missiles inevitably increased.[22] As General Arnold pointed out in his final *War Report*, "The danger zone of modern war is not restricted to battle lines and adjacent areas but extends to the innermost parts of a nation. No one is immune from the ravages of war."[23] "Under atomic bomb warfare," warned Jacob Viner, "the soldier in the army would be safer than his wife and children in their urban home."[24] This mutual vulnerability, which has been characteristic of the nuclear age, provides the basis for mutual deterrence.

It was widely predicted that the next major war involving the United States would begin with a massive surprise atomic attack against the continental U.S. from across the oceans (in most cases this was apparently an implicit reference to the Soviet Union). Again, World War II experience set the precedent. According to Professor J. Robert Oppenheimer:

The pattern of the use of atomic weapons was set at Hiroshima. They are weapons of aggression, of surprise, and of terror. If they are ever used again it may well be by the thousands. . . . It is a weapon for aggressors, and the elements of surprise and of terror are as intrinsic to it as are the fissionable nuclei.[25]

Pearl Harbor provided another spectacular example of the possibilities of surprise attack. Liddell Hart reminded his readers "that 'Port Arthur' in 1904 was followed by 'Pearl Harbor' in 1941, and we should not over-look the possibilities of a third trick in the series."[26] Visualizing a "push-button" war in which hundreds of enemy rockets would descend on the largest U.S. cities, Dr. Brown argued that "The 'Pearl Harbor' of the future will reduce the one of the past to insignificance."[27] Professor Ridenour went so far as to state that "war, or even a new phase of a war already in progress, *always* starts with a Pearl Harbor kind of attack."[28]

The fear of surprise atomic attack was not restricted to nongovern-mental civilian analysts. In his April 1945 memorandum to the President, Secretary of War Stimson cautioned that in the future:

Such a weapon may be constructed in secret and used suddenly and effectively with devastating power by a willful nation or group against an unsuspecting nation or group of much greater size and material power. With its aid even a very powerful unsuspecting nation might be conquered within a very few days by a very much smaller one.[29]

General H. H. Arnold, commander of the U.S. Army Air Force, evidently shared the same nightmare, warning that:

Future attack upon the United States may well be without warning. . . . Today many modern war devices of great destructive power can be built piecemeal and under cover. Sub-assemblies might be secretly made in underground laboratories, and assembled into an annihilating war machine. War may descend upon us by thousands of robots passing unannounced across our shorelines.[30]

The Secretary of State's Committee on Atomic Energy predicted that international suspicion would be "accentuated by the unusual character-istics of atomic bombs, namely their devastating effect as a surprise weapon, that is, a weapon secretly developed and used without warning."[31]

This perception complicated efforts at international control of atomic energy.

In May 1947, the President's Advisory Committee on Universal Training, chaired by Dr. Karl T. Compton, issued its report emphasizing the urgency of universal military training (UMT) as well as increasing strategic air power. Despite its stress on the continuing need for conventional forces, the report repeated the prevalent point of view regarding the most likely scenario for the outbreak of the next war:

The "sneak attack" of the type delivered upon our forces at Pearl Harbor is made vastly more probable by the increased range of aircraft and the enormous destructive capacity of atomic weapons. . . . The signal for the start of a war against us will, it is to be expected, be a large-scale, long-distance onslaught with atomic explosives against our principal centers of population and production.[32]

As the foregoing quotes demonstrate, it was widely believed that cities and industrial centers would be the primary targets of a nuclear attack. This appears to have been an implicit assumption in some cases, probably based largely on the Allied targeting strategies of the World War II strategic bombing campaign. "Today, Japanese and German cities lie in ruins," noted General Arnold, "but they merely suggest the vast destruction that can be done with the weapons of tomorrow. The first target of a potential aggressor might well be our industrial system or our major centers of population."[33]

Beginning with the British raids on German cities in 1941 and culminating with Hiroshima and Nagasaki, massive strategic bombing of the enemy's cities was a central element of Anglo-American military strategy throughout the war.[34] In fact, as much or more destruction, both in terms of casualties and loss of property, was caused by the conventional bombing raids on Tokyo and Dresden than by the atomic bombs dropped on Hiroshima and Nagasaki.[35] To some observers, atomic weapons may have represented simply a more efficient or lethal means of achieving the same ends, but many experts, shocked by the destructive power of atomic bombs, perceived a clear distinction between conventional and atomic munitions. Yet the strategic focus remained on countervalue, not counterforce, targets. As Robert Oppenheimer pointed out, "Since the United States and Britain in this past war were willing to engage in mass demolition and incendiary raids against civilian centers and did in fact use atomic weapons against primarily civilian targets, there would seem little valid hope that such use would not be made in any future major war."[36]

During World Wars I and II, the ability of the United States to mobilize its vast unharmed industrial base was clearly a major factor in the Allied victories. Hence, numerous authors suggested that U.S. industry might well be a major target in an enemy first strike.[37] In testimony before the Compton Commission, Lt. General J. Lawton Collins made the dire prediction that:

We could expect that the war would start very suddenly and come through the air and that the enemy would try to eliminate the United States at the outset, not making the same mistake as last time of taking on somebody else first and allowing us to prepare. The attack would be primarily at the great cities and would cause great destruction both to physical structures and the people. . . . The atomic bomb would probably be used against cities in preference to military targets.[38]

Moreover, as Bernard Brodie phrased it, "for some time to come, the primary targets for the atomic bomb will be cities. One does not shoot rabbits with elephant guns, especially if there are elephants available."[39] The immense destructive power of atomic bombs and their large initial expense made cities their most likely targets. According to Jacob Viner:

The bomb has a minimum size, and in this size it is, and will remain, too expensive—or too scarce, whether expensive or not—to be used against minor targets. Its targets, therefore, must be primarily cities, and its military effectiveness must reside primarily in its capacity to destroy urban population and productive facilities.[40]

J. Robert Oppenheimer agreed, pointing out that the atomic bomb's "disproportionate power of destruction is greatest in strategic bombardment: In destroying centers of population, and population itself, and in destroying industry."[41]

Some of the more vivid predictions of vast destruction to U.S. cities may have been prompted by the desire to impress upon the public consciousness the urgency either of developing international control mechanisms or of increasing expenditures for strategic air power. In arguing for international control, the Secretary of State's Committee on Atomic Energy cited "the really revolutionary character of these weapons, particularly as weapons of strategic bombardment aimed at the destruction of enemy cities and the eradication of their populations" and warned of "the probable horrors of a war in which atomic weapons were used by both combatants against the cities of their enemy."[42] On the other hand, General Arnold also graphically described the vulnerability of our cities, but concluded that "the atomic weapon thus makes offensive and defensive Air Power in a state of immediate readiness the primary requisite of national survival."[43] This link between the security of U.S. cities and the size of the Air Force budget was emphasized repeatedly in the President's Air Policy Commission Report (the Finletter Report) of January 1, 1948.[44]

The lack of an effective defense, the aggressive nature of atomic weapons and the likely targeting of cities all confirmed that there could be no victor in a nuclear war. Frederick S. Dunn cogently described this dilemma of modern war as follows:

In the pre-atomic days of the 1940's things had been bad enough, but one did not have to contemplate very seriously the probable annihilation of both victor and vanquished. Now, even the strongest states were faced with the prospect that they might no longer be able, by their own strength, to save their cities from destruction. . . . It was becoming very hard to see how a tolerable war could be fought any more. Unless atomic warfare could be limited, no single state, no matter how strong its military forces might be, could be at all certain to avoid being mortally wounded in a future war. There was not and very likely would not be a sure defence against atomic attack, or any reliable way of keeping bombs away from a nation's territory. A great power might, it is true, by building up to the limit of its strength, have a good chance of winning a war in the end, but what good was that if in the meantime the urban population of the nation had been wiped out?[45]

"That there can be no 'victor' in atomic war is so plain," concluded the Compton Report, "that we must continue to focus all our statesmanship on the attainment of a trustworthy program for eliminating the employment of atomic weapons."[46]

Not every observer concluded that the development of weapons capable of destroying mankind would inevitably lead to their widespread use in future war. In fact, the very destructiveness of these weapons hopefully might restrain national leaders from ever employing them in combat. B. H. Liddell Hart expressed this hope:

Where both sides possess atomic power, "*total* warfare" makes nonsense. . . . An unlimited war waged with atomic power would be worse than nonsense, it would be mutually suicidal. That conclusion does not necessarily mean that warfare will completely disappear. But, unless the belligerent leaders are crazy, it is likely that any future warfare will be less unrestrained and more subject to mutually agreed rules.[47]

Indeed, the assumption of rationality on the part of opposing national leaders eventually became a major issue in theoretical assessments of the durability of mutual deterrence. Harrison Brown also acknowledged the possibility "that all nations may become so frightened at the probable consequences of using atomic weapons that they will, for a time at least, wage war according to the standard methods," but he described the hypothetical situation as "metastable" in that "sooner or later, one of the nations, close to defeat, will become desperate" and resort to atomic weapons.[48]

Only two months after Hiroshima, Professor Jacob Viner (evidently the first of many economists to venture into the realm of nuclear strategy) questioned the likelihood of "a war which opened with atomic-bomb attacks on both sides":

A much more plausible hypothesis is that in a war between two fairly equally matched states possessed of atomic bombs at the start; each side would decide that it had nothing to gain and a great deal to lose from reciprocal use of the bombs, and that unilateral use was not attainable. The bombs would then either never be used or would be used only when one of the countries, in the face of imminent defeat, falls back upon their use in a last desperate effort to escape a dictated peace.[49]

Professor Viner also suggested that superiority in nuclear weapons was a meaningless concept, since "a superior bomb cannot neutralize the inferior bomb of an enemy" and "superiority in efficiency affects chiefly the fineness of the dust to which it reduces the city upon which it is dropped."[50] The debate over the meaning and importance of nuclear superiority has continued to this very day.

The perceived likelihood of mutual destruction in any future war involving nuclear weapons provided the best possible rationale for mutual deterrence. This vital relationship was widely recognized in numerous publications within months after the dropping of the first atomic bombs and years before a foreign power acquired these weapons of mass destruction. Bernard Brodie summarized the concept well:

If the aggressor state must fear retaliation, it will know that even if it is the victor it will suffer a degree of physical destruction incomparably greater than that suffered by any defeated nation of history, incomparably greater, that is, than that suffered by Germany in the recent war. Under those circumstances no victory, even if guaranteed in advance—which it never is—would be worth the price. The threat of retaliation does not have to be 100 percent certain; it is sufficient if there is a good chance of it, or if there is belief that there is a good chance of it. The prediction is more important than the fact.[51]

This analysis was particularly remarkable in its distinction between the perception and the reality of the threat of retaliation. Dr. Brodie quite rightly understood that the key to deterrence was convincing the opponent that he would suffer disastrous consequences from launching a first strike.

Other analysts stressed that the retaliatory forces should be kept at full readiness, prepared to respond instantaneously to an enemy attack. According to Frederick S. Dunn:

It happens that the bomb is well adapted to the technique of retaliation. One must assume that so long as bombs exist at all, the states possessing them will hold themselves in readiness at all times for instant retaliation on the fullest possible scale in the event of an atomic attack. The result would be that any potential violator of a limitation agreement would have the terrifying contemplation that not only would he lose his cities immediately on starting an attack, but that his transportation and communication systems would doubtless be gone and his industrial capacity for producing the materials of war would be ruined. If in spite of all this he still succeeded in winning the war, he would find that he had conquered nothing but a blackened ruin.[52]

Dr. Brown agreed, recommending that " 'Retaliation' bombs must be prepared for instantaneous action against any nation attacking us. We must realize that this measure is not a defense; it is simply a deterrent that might possibly delay, for a while, an enemy attack from a distance."[53] This recommendation is fully consistent with the more recent practice of maintaining a portion of the SAC bombers either in the air or on alert status at all times.

Modern deterrence theory argues that in order to provide a credible deterrent, a nation's strategic deterrent forces must be capable of absorbing an opponent's counterforce first strike and replying with devastating force. According to the U.S. Strategic Bombing Survey, "A wise military establishment will make sure—by dispersal, concealment, protection, and constant readiness of its forces—that no single blow or series of blows from an enemy can cripple its ability to strike back the same way or to repel accompanying attacks from other air, ground, or sea forces."[54] Professor Viner advocated dispersal as a means of reducing the vulnerability of atomic weapons and production facilities.[55] Ansley Coale perceived that "the ability to deliver and to absorb are of course interrelated: it is particularly important that the means of attack be capable of surviving assault."[56] In particular, he specified that "to prevent attack, then, the United States would make sure that after receiving the strongest assault that could be launched upon it, it would remain capable of retaliating with a full-scale, several-thousand-bomb counterattack."[57] Even the consumers of the *Reader's Digest* were informed by Francis Vivian Drake that continued U.S. "supremacy in atomic weapons" would provide "the glimmer of a great hope that atomic bombardment may never be used against us."[58]

The unpublished U.S. Army General Staff study, as described by Joseph and Stewart Alsop, called for the establishment of "an immense, invulnerable mechanism of retaliation, which will be instantaneously set off by the first warning of enemy attack."[59] This fire-on-warning system would consist "of a great chain of special rocket installations throughout the United States" which would "be dug deep into the ground for protection against attack."[60] Moreover, these "concrete caverns will house a complete apparatus of destruction, always in full readiness."[61] The report evidently contained a remarkably detailed and prescient description of the hardened U.S. ICBM installations which were not constructed until some fifteen years later.

The theory of deterrence, as enunciated by these early nuclear strategists, was not immediately endorsed unanimously within the U.S. government.[62] After all, at that time the U.S. possessed a monopoly on atomic weapons and was unlikely to deprecate their potential military value in defense of U.S. national security. However, air power advocates quickly adopted the concept, which provided a rationale for a larger strategic air force. Only two months after Hiroshima and Nagasaki, General Arnold endorsed deterrence as the basis for U.S. strategic policy:

[The United States] must recognize that real security against atomic weapons in the future will rest on our ability to take immediate offensive action with overwhelming force. It must be apparent to a potential aggressor that an attack on the United States would be immediately followed by an immensely devastating air-atomic attack on him.[63]

Two years later, the President's Air Policy Commission Report (the Fin-letter Report) repeatedly stressed this theme in justifying the need for large increases in the Air Force budget.[64] The U.S. Strategic Bombing Survey recognized that "As defense weapons, atomic bombs are useful primarily as warnings, as threats of retaliation which will restrain a potential aggressor from their use as from the use of poison gas or bio-logical warfare."[65] Similarly, the Alsop brothers quoted the U.S. Army General Staff report as concluding that "the power to retaliate is the best deterrent of attack."[66]

These early writings perceptively outlined the major tenets of deter-rence theory long before these concepts became official policy. Yet, many important questions regarding deterrence were not considered by these pioneers in nuclear strategic theory. For instance, what range of potential security threats could be effectively deterred by strategic nuclear weapons? Can nuclear deterrent forces compensate for conventional military weaknesses? How large a force of what configuration provides an adequate deterrent? Can the Soviet Union be deterred from expanding Communist influence? How can strategic threats be most effectively and credibly communicated to the adversary? During the 1950's and 1960's many of these questions were analyzed at length by the growing body of strategic theorists.

Many of the early strategists tended to exaggerate the immediate pros-pects for the development and large-scale procurement of intercontinental delivery vehicles, particularly rockets, by the U.S. and its adversaries. Yet they demonstrated great foresight regarding the future role of strategic nuclear weapons and persuasively argued for an emphasis on deterrence rather than defense. Their conclusion that there does not exist an adequate defense against a concerted nuclear attack has been reinforced by subse-quent technological developments. Efforts to develop effective active defenses have not kept pace with offensive developments, such as the tremendous increase in the number of delivery vehicles, the massive deployment of MIRVs, and the development of sea-based deterrent forces, including both ballistic and cruise missiles. In the U.S., passive defenses have proven to be either infeasible, as in the case of the dispersal of industry and population, or very unpopular, as were civil defense and shelter programs. The superiority of offense over defense was officially sanctioned by the 1972 Soviet-American treaty limiting ABM deploy-ments.

However, the early assumption that a nuclear war is likely to begin with a massive attack on cities has been challenged by the advocates of city avoidance and selective counterforce targeting. Recent technological advances have considerably increased the potential accuracies of U.S. and Soviet ICBMs, and this trend has encouraged counterforce advocates to claim that a selective strike against the opponent's strategic forces would cause a minimum of civilian casualties. Yet a recent Department of Defense study concludes that the number of American casualties from a limited counterforce strike by the Soviet Union would probably reach into the tens of millions.[67] Thus, though the early strategists were mistaken in not considering the possibility that national leaders might choose to concentrate a nuclear strike on military targets rather than cities, they correctly perceived that the inevitably great number of casualties would make it very difficult to limit a nuclear exchange and quite impossible to envision a meaningful "victory."

Yet many questions remain concerning how a nuclear conflict, perhaps begun by accident, might be limited and then terminated. If deterrence should fail, U.S. and Soviet leaders ought to share more understanding of how to minimize the loss of life and destruction of property. Could a new mutual deterrence relationship be established after the initial strategic exchange? Could either side accept a stalemate after incurring such great losses, or would both sides blindly continue to pursue a military "victory"? What political objectives would be considered adequate to justify the costs, and how might these objectives be modified during the conflict? What role would conventional forces play? For instance, would there be any attempt to occupy the enemy's territory?

Equally difficult and hypothetical questions might be posed regarding the postwar environment. Would national authorities remain to cope with the casualties and rebuild the society, or would anarchy, local government, or world government be more likely alternatives? Would those countries least affected by the conflict dominate the postwar world? Would the prospects for global disarmament be improved by the terrible demonstration of the ultimate futility of weapons of mass destruction?

Nuclear war endings are certainly unpleasant to think about and difficult to conceptualize. But even the most ardent supporters of deterrence do not argue that the system is fail-proof, and, if deterrence should fail, these seemingly hypothetical questions become urgent issues of survival.

These questions should be discussed widely in public forums, rather than only by a few experts in highly classified reports. Unfortunately, these issues do not disappear simply by ignoring them.[68] Realistic evaluations of nuclear war endings would not undermine deterrence by making nuclear war seem more acceptable, but instead would illustrate the horrors of nuclear conflicts and thus might well spur efforts towards arms control and disarmament.

The early post–World War II theorists, largely basing their analysis on the lessons of strategic bombing during the war, very persuasively defined the parameters of strategic theory which have been largely adhered to ever since. Current popular conceptions of nuclear warfare are, to a great extent, simply refinements of arguments developed intuitively some thirty years ago. Although several of these fundamental concepts still appear to be valid, their enormous influence has tended to direct attention away from the study of nuclear war endings.

NOTES

1. Herman Kahn has been the chief exception. For instance, see *On Thermonuclear War* (Princeton: Princeton University Press, 1960), *Thinking About the Unthinkable* (New York: Horizon Press, 1962), *On Escalation: Metaphors and Scenarios* (New York: Frederick A. Praeger, 1965), "Issues of Thermonuclear War Termination," in "How Wars End," *Annals of the American Academy of Political and Social Science,* November 1970, ed. William T. R. Fox, and, with William Pfaff and Edmund Stillman, "War Termination, Issues and Concepts" (Harmon-on-Hudson, N.Y.: Hudson Institute, June 1968).

2. A thorough discussion of this issue can be found in Glenn H. Snyder, *Deterrence and Defense: Toward a Theory of National Security* (Princeton: Princeton University Press, 1961).

3. Among the more prominent treatments of this issue are Richard Leghorn, "No Need to Bomb Cities to Win War," *U.S. News and World Report,* 38 (January 28, 1955), 78-94, William W. Kaufmann, "Limited Warfare," in *Military Policy and National Security,* ed. Kaufmann (Princeton: Princeton University Press, 1956), Arnold Wolfers, "Could a War in Europe Be Limited?" *Yale Review,* 45 (Winter 1956), 214-28, Robert E. Osgood, *Limited War: The Challenge to American Strategy* (Chicago: University of Chicago Press, 1957), Henry A. Kissinger, *Nuclear Weapons and Foreign Policy* (New York: Harper and Brothers, 1957), Thomas C. Schelling, "Bargaining, Communication and Limited War," *Journal of Conflict Resolution,* 1 (March 1957), 19-36, Klaus Knorr, ed., *Nato and American Security* (Princeton: Princeton University Press, 1959), and Morton H. Halperin, *Limited War in the Nuclear Age* (New York: John Wiley and Sons, 1963).

4. U.S., President, *Public Papers of the Presidents of the United States* (Washington, D.C.: Office of the *Federal Register,* National Archives and Records Service), Harry S. Truman, 1945, pp. 472-73.

5. Ivan A. Getting, "Facts About Defense," and Henry DeWolf Smyth, "The Pattern of Destruction," both in *The Nation,* 161 (December 22, 1945), 703-704

and 701–702, respectively. Another well-known physicist, Louis N. Ridenour, reached the same conclusion in an article entitled "There Is No Defense," in *One World or None*, ed. Dexter Masters and Katharine Way (New York: McGraw-Hill Book Co., 1946), pp. 33–38.

6.   Caryl P. Haskins, "Atomic Energy and American Foreign Policy," *Foreign Affairs*, 24 (July 1946), 591; Harrison Brown, *Must Destruction Be Our Destiny?* (New York: Simon and Schuster, 1946), p. 61; Bernard Brodie, "Implications for Military Policy," in *The Absolute Weapon: Atomic Power and World Order*, ed. Brodie (New York: Harcourt, Brace and Co., 1946), p. 78.

7.   Winfield W. Riefler, preface to *The Problem of Reducing Vulnerability to Atomic Bombs*, by Ansley J. Coale (Princeton: Princeton University Press, 1947), p. viii. In contrast to the apparent unanimity among scientists, U.S. public opinion seemed to be divided on this issue, with many people believing that an effective defense would be developed by the United States. See Leonard S. Cottrell, Jr., and Sylvia Eberhart, *American Opinion on World Affairs in the Atomic Age* (Princeton: Princeton University Press, 1948), pp. 18–19, and Sylvia Eberhart, "How the American People Feel About the Atomic Bomb," *Bulletin of the Atomic Scientists*, 3 (June 1947), 146–149, 168.

8.   Emergency Committee of Atomic Scientists, "A Statement," *Bulletin of the Atomic Scientists*, 3 (June 1947), 1.

9.   U.S., Department of State, Secretary of State's Committee on Atomic Energy, *A Report on the International Control of Atomic Energy*, Pubn. No. 2498 (March 16, 1946), p. 2.

10.   Joseph and Stewart Alsop. "Your Flesh Should Creep," *Saturday Evening Post*, 219 (July 13, 1946), 44.

11.   U.S. Strategic Bombing Survey, "The Atomic Bomb and Our Cities," *Bulletin of the Atomic Scientists*, 2 (August 1, 1946), 30.

12.   Brown, *Destiny*, p. 10.

13.   Francis Vivian Drake, "Let's Be Realistic About the Atom Bomb," *Reader's Digest*, December 1945, p. 109.

14.   Henry L. Stimson and McGeorge Bundy, *On Active Service in Peace and War* (New York: Harper and Brothers, 1948), p. 635.

15.   Coale, *Vulnerability*, pp. 86–93. Louis Ridenour presented a similar analysis in "No Defense."

16.   B. H. Liddell Hart, *The Revolution in Warfare* (London: Faber and Faber, Ltd., 1946), p. 84.

17.   Brown, *Destiny* p. 31. Also see Drake, "Realistic," p. 108.

18.   Brodie, "War in Atomic Age," p. 44. Dr. J. R. Oppenheimer and General H. H. Arnold reached the same conclusion through a comparative analysis of the cost of destroying an enemy city with conventional and atomic bombs according to U.S. experience in World War II. Oppenheimer, "The New Weapon: The Turn of the Screw," *One World or None*, pp. 24–25, and Arnold, "Air Force in the Atomic Age," *One World or None*, pp. 26–30. See also Haskins, "Atomic Energy," pp. 598–599.

19.   Brown, *Destiny*, p. 47; see also p. 62.

20.   For example, see Robert S. McNamara, *The Essence of Security: Reflections in Office* (New York: Harper and Row, 1968), pp. 63–66, and various congressional hearings, especially U.S., Congress, Senate, Subcommittee on International Organization and Disarmament Affairs of the Committee on Foreign Relations, *Strategic and Foreign Policy Implications of ABM Systems*, 3 parts, 91st Cong., 1st sess., 1969, and U.S., Congress, Senate, Subcommittee on Arms Control, International Law and Organization of the Committee on Foreign Relations, *ABM, MIRV, SALT and the Nuclear Arms Race*, 91st Cong., 2nd sess., 1970.

21.   For instance, see Drake, "Realistic," p. 110, Brown, *Destiny*, p. 30, Brodie, "War in Atomic Age," p. 31, Smyth, "Destruction," p. 701, Getting, "Defense," p. 704, General Arnold, *Third War Report*, pp. 463–464, and Potomacus, "Strategy in the Atomic Age," *New Republic*, November 5, 1945, p. 601.

22. For example, see Alsops, "Your Flesh Should Creep," pp. 591 and 598, Nigel Tangye, "Flying Bombs and Rockets: This Time and Next," *Foreign Affairs* 24 (October 1945), 40 and 49, and, pre-Hiroshima, Grayson Kirk, "National Power and Foreign Policy," *Foreign Affairs*, 23 (July 1945), 621.

23. General Arnold, *Third War Report*, p. 452.

24. Jacob Viner, "The Implications of the Atomic Bomb for International Relations," *Proceedings of the American Philosophical Society*, 90 (January 1946), 53.

25. J. R. Oppenheimer, "Atomic Weapons," *Proceedings of the American Philosophical Society*, 90 (January 1946), 9. Henry Smyth concluded that war in the atomic age "would almost surely mean surprise attack." Smyth, "Destruction," p. 702.

26. Liddell Hart, *Revolution in Warfare*, p. 84.

27. Brown, *Destiny*, p. 33.

28. Ridenour, "No Defense," p. 37.

29. Stimson and Bundy, p. 635. A similar concern over small nations gaining atomic power is expressed by Frederick S. Dunn, "The Common Problem," in *The Absolute Weapon*, p. 5.

30. General Arnold, *Third War Report*, pp. 452–454.

31. Secretary of State's Committee on Atomic Energy, *Report*, p. 4. Joseph and Stewart Alsop, in reporting the conclusions of the U.S. Army General Staff study, warned that "the very nature of atomic warfare will place a heavy premium upon striking the first blow." Alsops, "Your Flesh Should Creep," p. 44.

32. U.S., President, President's Advisory Commission on Universal Training, *A Program for National Security*, May 29, 1947 (Washington, D.C.: Government Printing Office, 1947), p. 8.

33. General Arnold, *Third War Report*, p. 454. Also see Potomacus, "Strategy," p. 601.

34. Quester, *Deterrence Before Hiroshima*, pp. 105–171.

35. See David Irving, *The Destruction of Dresden* (New York: Holt, Rinehart and Winston, 1963), p.p. 9, 11, and 210, William Craig, *Fall of Japan* (New York: Dial Press, 1967), pp. 20–26, U.S., Air Force, Historical Division, *The Army Air Forces in World War II*, ed. by Wesley Frank Craven and James Lea Cate (Chicago: University of Chicago Press, 1948), U.S., Strategic Bombing Survey, Medical Division, *The Effects of Atomic Bombs on Health and Medical Services in Hiroshima and Nagasaki* (Washington, D.C.: Government Printing Office, March 1947), and U.S., Strategic Bombing Survey, Urban Areas Division, *Effects of Air Attack on Urban Complex Tokyo-Kawasaki-Yokohama* (Washington, D.C.: Government Printing Office, June 1947).

36. Oppenheimer, "Turn of the Screw," p. 25.

37. For example, see Brown, *Destiny*, pp. 52–54, General Arnold, *Third War Report*, p. 453, Potomacus, "Strategy," p. 601, and Alsops, "Your Flesh Should Creep," p. 44.

38. President's Advisory Commission on Universal Training, *Program*, p. 13.

39. Brodie, "War in Atomic Age," pp. 46–47.

40. Viner, "Implications," p. 53.

41. Oppenheimer, "Turn of the Screw," p. 25.

42. Secretary of State's Committee on Atomic Energy, *Report*, p. 1.

43. General Arnold, *Third War Report*, p. 464.

44. U.S., President, President's Air Policy Commission, *Survival in the Air Age* (Washington, D.C.: Government Printing Office, 1948).

45. Dunn, "Common Problem," pp. 4–5.

46. President's Advisory Commission on Universal Training, *Program*, p. 18.

47. Liddell Hart, *Revolution in Warfare*, p. 85.

48. Brown, *Destiny*, pp. 52-53.

49. Viner, "Implications," p. 54.

50. Ibid., p. 53.

51. Brodie, "Implications," p. 74.
52. Dunn, "Common Problem," p. 16.
53. Brown, *Destiny*, p. 42; see also p. 34.
54. U.S. Strategic Bombing Survey, "Atomic Bomb and Our Cities," p. 30. The Compton and Finletter Reports also advocated the development of an air force capable both of retaliation (deterrence) and of blunting the enemy attack (active defense).
55. Viner, "Implications," pp. 53–54.
56. Coale, *Vulnerability*, p. 54.
57. Ibid., p. 50. For his suggestions on how this might be accomplished, see pp. 55–60. He provides an interesting, but somewhat inconclusive, discussion of the meaning of "victory" in a nuclear war, pp. 50–55. He admits that "the goal of winning a war in which quantities of atomic bombs are employed by each side is not one to inspire much enthusiasm. However, if international limitation of weapons proves unattainable, enthusiastic preparations to win might be the best course remaining to escape attack" (p. 50) Thus, deterrence might be attained through preparing for "victory."
58. Drake, "Realistic," p. 110.
59. Alsops, "Your Flesh Should Creep," p. 47.
60. Ibid.
61. Ibid.
62. Although there appeared to be general acceptance of the need for strong retaliatory air forces to discourage an enemy attack, there were apparent disagreements concerning the relative role to be played in the future by conventional forces (land armies and navies). This debate was reflected in differences between the Compton and Finletter Reports. For an insightful analysis of these positions, see P. M. S. Blackett, *Fear, War, and the Bomb* (New York: Whittlesey House, 1948), pp. 229–236. A fuller exposition of Army and Navy views can be found in "War Department Thinking on the Atomic Bomb," *Bulletin of the Atomic Scientists*, 3 (June 1947), 150–155, 168, Bernard Brodie, "Navy Department Thinking on the Atomic Bomb," *Bulletin of the Atomic Scientists*, 3 (July 1947), 177-80, 198-99, and Bernard Brodie. "A Critique of Army and Navy Thinking on the Atomic Bomb," *Bulletin of the Atomic Scientists*, 3 (August 1947), 207-210.
63. General Arnold, *Third War Report*, p. 464. See also his article "Air Force in the Atomic Age," *One World or None*, pp. 31–32.
64. President's Air Policy Commission, *Survival*, pp. 6–27.
65. U.S. Strategic Bombing Survey, "Atomic Bomb and Our Cities," p. 30
66. Alsops, "Your Flesh Should Creep," p. 47.
67. Leslie H. Gelb, "The Changing Estimates of Nuclear Horror," *New York Times*, October 19, 1975, and John W. Finney, "Pentagon Raises Atom Toll Count," *New York Times*, September 17, 1975.
68. For a more extensive discussion of this point, see Herman Kahn, *Thinking About the Unthinkable*, esp. chapt. 1, "In Defense of Thinking." Surveys of the open literature suggest that public and scholarly interest in nuclear war has been declining remarkably. Rob Paarlberg, "Forgetting about the Unthinkable," *Foreign Policy*, no. 10 (Spring 1973), pp. 132–140.

Section II

VICTORY AND DEFEAT

BERENICE A. CARROLL

3
VICTORY AND DEFEAT:
The Mystique of Dominance

Victory and defeat are strikingly symbiotic conceptions. *Webster's International Dictionary* offers only one substantive meaning for victory: "the overcoming of an enemy in battle, or of an antagonist in any contest; a gaining of superiority in any struggle; conquest; triumph; the opposite of defeat." To conquer, we learn elsewhere, derives originally from the root *quaerere*, to seek (*viz.* "quest"); it once meant "to procure by effort, to acquire," and it still has meanings independent of any antagonist—e.g., to conquer difficulties or temptation, to overcome obstacles by mental or moral power. But the primary contemporary meaning of *conquest* also requires a defeated opponent—still more, an opponent defeated by violent means: "to gain or acquire by force of arms; to take possession by violent means; to gain dominion over; to subjugate; . . . to vanquish" (*Webster's International Dictionary*, 1959:2842,566).

The ancient images of victory and defeat are highly personalized: the victor stands erect and triumphant on the field of battle, the defeated bends helpless at his feet. The victor is welcomed home in triumphal procession, the defeated drag along in chains, touching their foreheads to the ground. In its extreme form, victorious force is, as Simone Weil argued, that which "turns anybody who is subjected to it into a *thing*" (Weil, 1956:3). Thus Achilles, in the final battles described in the *Iliad*, slaughters the Trojans like animals, indifferent alike to valor and pleading, reducing them all to steaming meat:

> So saying, he thrust his spear .
> Through the neck of Dryops, who fell at his feet . . . .
> Then Alastor's son Tros—he reached for the knees of Achilles,
> Pleading with him to take him alive. . . .
> Tros tried to hug the man's knees, jabbering a prayer
> To be spared, but Achilles thrust his sword in at the liver,
> Which slipped from the wound as the dark blood quickly welled out
> And slithered down to drip from his chest. Soon all
> Became dark and he fainted. And on went Achilles to stab
> His bronze spear-point from ear to ear through Mulius' skull,
> And then to strike Echeclus full on the head
> With his dark-hilted sword, where at the whole blade was left smoking
> With blood, as purple death came down on his eyes
> And powerful fate embraced him. Next, he jabbed
> His bronze-pointed spear through the arm of Deucalion, right
> Where the tendons join at the elbow, and he stood there
> With his arm too heavy to lift, awaiting the death
> Coming on, and Achilles, whipping his sword through the neck
> Of the warrior, swept his helmeted head far away,
> Causing marrow to spurt from his spine and his corpse to lie
> Stretched out on the ground.
>
> (Homer, 1963:420-421)

Finally the great hero Hector, slain at last by Achilles, is constrained to beg with his dying breaths for the return of his body to the Trojans for proper burial, but Achilles roughly refuses, insisting that "dogs and birds shall devour you." Acting on his words, he strips the armor from Hector's corpse, and the Greeks run up to stare and scoff and mutilate the body: "nor did a man approach him without inflicting a wound in his flesh." Achilles then sets about the final reduction of Hector to a thing:

> Piercing behind the tendons
> Of both of his feet between heel and ankle, he pulled through
> And tied leather thongs, and bound them fast to his chariot,
> Leaving the head to drag. Then lifting the famous
> Armor aboard, he mounted the car himself
> And lashed the team on, and they unreluctant took off
> At a gallop. And dust billowed up on either side
> Of the dragging Hector, as his black hair trailed out
> In the dirt and the once so handsome head was defiled
> With foul dust.
>
> (Homer, 1963:420-421)

(One is reminded of some photographs of bodies dragging behind tanks or jeeps in Vietnam.)

Other images of the conquered are portrayed in the *Iliad*: Hecuba and Andromache, lamenting Hector's death and fated to be enslaved by the Greeks, and King Priam, who lives to find himself a suppliant before his son's slayer, pleading for the return of Hector's body:

> Great Priam came in unnoticed
> By any, till coming up close to Achilles he threw
> His arms round his knees and kissed his dread hands, the murderous
> Hands that had killed so many of his precious sons.[1]
>
> (Homer, 1963:506)

Priam lives, but the Trojan defeat has reduced him to abasement before the murderer of his own sons.

The images of defeat and victory in modern warfare are somewhat less personalized. Perhaps Hitler entering Vienna to cheering crowds in 1938 , and his presumed charred remains dug up in the rubble of East Berlin in 1945 carry forward the ancient tradition: the victor in triumphal procession, the defeated reduced to a thing. But on the whole, modern images of the moment of victory and defeat have a less individualized character: murals of mass celebration or mass despair, snapshots of uniformed men (civilian and military) signing surrender documents.

Still, the symbiosis between victory and defeat remains as central in the image of modern war endings as it was in the ancient epics, though displaced from the personal to the collective. The victor requires the defeated; otherwise the victory is meaningless. Hector cannot be simply eliminated: he must live again as a heroic figure in Greek legend and poetry, else the victory perishes with the victim. The nations of Europe cannot simply disappear under Hitler's rule: they must be made to serve the New Order, else the victor has conquered nothing. The defeated does not require the victor in the same sense, but the status of defeat is defined by a relationship to the victor. The core of this relationship is the assertion of dominance on the part of the victor, submission on the part of the defeated. The symbiosis is complete: without dominance, there is no submission; without submission, there can be no dominance.

This conclusion may seem truistic, perhaps even tautological. But the symbiosis between victory and defeat has not been fully recognized or understood. Prevailing conceptions of victory in modern warfare depend upon—and reinforce—a mystique of dominance as an autonomous force. This is not to deny that dominance is a reality, but rather to suggest that it is not an *independent* reality, and that a substantial component of its force lies in widespread acceptance of its mystique.

I have argued elsewhere that the war system is inherent in the power system, that is, the system of power as dominance (Carroll, 1972). If that is true, then the demystification of dominance may be an essential step towards an end to the war system; and the demystification of victory and defeat may serve the same end.

It might be thought that there is no longer much need to demystify victory and defeat. One would think that they are already sufficiently demystified by the ironic reversals of fortune following World War II, in which the defeated powers today seem stronger and more prosperous than most of the "victors"; or by the evidently Pyrrhic character of any victory in a major thermonuclear war in the future; or by the inglorious, indeed shameful experiences of the Korean and Indochinese wars. But ancient images and categories are persistent. In the case of victory and defeat, they are reflected not only in conventional strategic doctrines, but also in much of the scholarly work that has been done in the field of war termination.

It is still quite generally held that wars do for the most part end in victory for one side, defeat for the other; stalemates and settlements with no discernible victor or defeated are regarded as relatively rare. This is not often stated as a general principle, and has sometimes been subjected to challenge.[2] Nevertheless it appears repeatedly, sometimes as an empirical observation on selected groups of wars, sometimes as an underlying assumption in the theoretical analysis of war endings.

Thus for example, Melvin Small and J. David Singer in *The Wages of War: 1816-1965, A Statistical Handbook* (1972), felt no difficulty in assigning victor or defeated status to the belligerents in all but one of fifty interstate wars and forty-three "extra-systemic" wars which they included in their study (Singer and Small, 1972:Ch.xiv).[3] Somewhat earlier, George Modelski had found that some four-fifths of 100 internal wars since 1900 ended in an "out-right win" or victory of one side or the other (Modelski, 1964:123). Though the empirical character of these determinations is open to serious question, no contrary data has yet been published. Moreover, the conclusion seems to draw support from the recent work of Robert F. Randle, *The Origins of Peace* (1973). Randle, in this extensive study of peace settlements, avoids any general statements regarding the prevalence of the victory-defeat syndrome in war endings. Nevertheless, his discussions of war outcomes and "factors for peace," and his descriptions of these points in selected groups of wars, rely heavily on the terms "victory" and "defeat," both for descriptive and for explanatory purposes. Though he does not say so, it is apparent that Randle felt it appropriate to assign victory or defeat in the majority of wars which he offers as examples.

Randle's frequent references to victory and defeat as explanations of "factors for peace" in sample wars place him closer than he might wish to those analysts who, in the tradition of H. A. Calahan, have held that the key to peace-making lies simply in the recognition of defeat on the part of the vanquished. Calahan wrote in 1944 that "war is pressed by the victor, but peace is made by the vanquished."[4] This position was echoed later by others, including Paul Kecskemeti and Lewis Coser, but its clearest theoretical statement appears in Nicholas S. Timasheff's *War and Revolution* (1965).

Timasheff viewed war as "a means of solving an inter-state conflict by measuring the relative strength of the parties." The relative strength of the parties, Timasheff argued, is a matter of "objective facts" which are real but not recognized at the outset. In the course of the war, however:

. . . estimates and expectations of the parties as to their relative strength, including the eventual intervention of neutrals, are gradually replaced by facts. *Through fighting it is established beyond reasonable doubt that one party is stronger than the other*; . . . . Then, one of the conditions of warfare, uncertainty as to relative strength, is eliminated. The immediate goal of war is attained; continuing it would no longer serve any reasonable purpose. Therefore, the war is over and the system composed of the fighting nations returns to peace.[5]

(Timasheff, 1965:204–205; italics added)

Timasheff goes on to make clear that the return to peace must take place through the initiative of the defeated.

One could not insist enough on the fact that, though the determinants of victory are objective facts, their assessment by the leaders of the parties to the conflict is a mental process which may lag behind the unfolding of the objective process. For quite a time, initial defeats may be considered as temporary setbacks only, and they may prove to be so. . . . But a moment comes when hope is lost . . . . the differential strength of the parties is established. Then, *it is for the weaker party to ask for the termination of hostilities* and thus to induce negotiations.

(Timasheff, 1965:217–218; italics added)

Finally, Timasheff concludes that in studying the "movement from war to peace" (i.e., war endings), the determination of victory is central:

> Therefore, the study of the causal background of the return of political systems from war to peace is tantamount to the study of the premises of victory and of the mechanism converting victory into peace.
>
> (Timasheff, 1965:205)

This assumes that there is necessarily a "real" correlation between the war outcome, in terms of who is *perceived* as victor and vanquished, and some independent measure(s) of who is "the stronger." The "victory" is taken to confirm, in itself, that the victor was stronger from the outset. This carries one step further the deterministic hypotheses of Kecskemeti and Coser which I have discussed elsewhere (Carroll, 1969) and makes explicit the circular aspect of the reasoning.

As suggested above, one must also question the empirical character of the available "data" on victory and defeat. In the case of Small and Singer, the determinations of victor and defeated nations were avowedly subjective, not based on "operational" criteria. Randle does not discuss the criteria for his references to victory and defeat. Modelski does specify one objective criterion for defining "outright win" in an internal war, namely, whether incumbents or insurgents emerge as the ruling government.

However, Modelski acknowledges that the term "outright win" requires qualification:

> . . . although coups, revolts, and revolutions often fail, the causes for which blood has been shed are seldom completely defeated. What we have called an "incumbents' win" amounts often to the destruction of the revolutionary core, its leaders and its "cadre"; the interests which the leaders stood for may, *more often than not*, be afterwards conciliated.
>
> (Modelski, 1964:124-125; italics added)

Among examples, Modelski notes the uprising in Madagascar which "was bloodily suppressed in 1947, but thirteen years later the island attained independence." Yet Madagascar appears in Modelski's list only as an "incumbents' win" in 1947-1948; its independence is not included in the list. It might be thought that Madagascar's achievement of independence was excluded because it did not at that time involve an armed insurrection. But on inspection, it appears that Modelski's list includes not only bloodless coups but even constitutional accessions to power, such as that of Hitler in 1933, so that the principles of selection and exclusion become rather obscure. Nor does Modelski's criterion for judging "outright win"—who governs in the outcome—take account of objectives which insurgents may be seeking other than ruling power. Thus the Russian Revolution of 1905 appears as an "incumbents' win," presumably because the monarchy did not fall, and reverted later to reaction. Yet for the most part the end of the monarchy was not in question among the insurgents' demands, and extensive concessions were initially won by extraordinary manifestations of spontaneous mass action. Even without taking into account the significant impact of the events of 1905 on those of 1917, to characterize the Revolution of 1905 as an "outright win" on the side of "the incumbents" is to stretch the historical data beyond the point of credibility.

How much or how little these considerations affect Modelski's conclusion that four-fifths of the internal "wars" between 1900 and 1962 ended in "outright wins" is impossible to say without detailed consideration of the individual cases. What is clear, however, is that to posit a *dichotomy* between victory and defeat is simplistic and imprecise, and obscures much more than it clarifies. Not only does it miss the symbiotic aspects of victory and defeat, but it misses even the more obvious variations in common usage of the terms. "Victory" is a highly elastic term, used to denote a wide variety of outcomes, whether military, political, or economic. Aside from several distinct interpretations in strictly military terms, "victory" may be interpreted as a relationship between the parties, as a relationship between war aims and war outcome, or as a relationship between gains and losses, in each case again in several distinct ways (Carroll, 1969; 305-306). "Victory" on one of these scales may not correspond with the outcomes on the other scales. Thus for example the Kingdom of Sardinia, by a negligible military contribution to the Allies in the Crimean War, won an important political victory, securing its leadership in the struggle for Italian unification; but England and France, through extensive military exertions, losses, and battle victories over Russia in the same war, won practically nothing. Indeed, the term "victory" is so elastic that Small and Singer felt it possible to include Poland among the "victors" in World War II, merely because she emerged from the war "on the winning side."

The dichotomous categorization of "victory" *versus* "defeat," based on a sliding scale or undefined criteria, or defined by some subjectively perceived "consensus of historians," is not only of dubious analytical value. Worse, it contributes to the confusion of ideas which feeds the mystique of dominance. Every minor political or territorial gain, every transitory battle success, every temporary suppression of revolutionary action, goes to swell the proud record of victory for the dominant, and the sad record of submission for the defeated.

To set out to demystify ancient and entrenched conceptions is a fairly presumptuous undertaking, certainly not to be accomplished within the scope of this paper. What we may do here is at most to touch on a few examples indicating possible approaches to the problem. At the outset, I would suggest that the demystification of victory and dominance cannot take place primarily by focusing attention on the victors and the dominant. Although one can point to a variety of disadvantages and costs to the victor, as some anti-imperialist and pacifist writings have long done, the prevailing tendency of historians and social scientists has been to focus attention upon those short-term gains which often are associated with "victory," and to emphasize the successful military or political techniques by which these gains were achieved. In effect this tends to reinforce the mystique by emphasizing the rewards, advantages and skills of dominance and, if only by omission, underlines the conventional image of the defeated as helpless and impotent. It is therefore necessary to turn attention here to the defeated, and to the nature and consequences of "defeat," to consider whether, or to what extent, the conventional image is valid.

It is seldom recognized that defeat can take forms as highly varied as "victory," carrying very different implications from case to case, or from one time to another. The British defeat of the Manchu Empire in the first Opium War involved quite minor concessions in 1842, but it came to carry a heavy overload of humiliating and disruptive implications in subsequent decades. The defeat of Algeria by the French, in the nineteenth century, or the defeat of France by the Germans, in 1940, involved the direct subjugation of the conquered populations to exploitative and oppressive foreign rule. The execution of Private Eddie Slovik in January 1945 resulted in his extinction as an individual human being, though it holds significantly different implications for us today.

One of the essential elements of the mystique of dominance is that the various possible meanings and levels of defeat are confounded into a single image. Thus any defeat, any obligation to make concessions, comes to be identified with surrender, or the posture of submission in general; submission, in turn, calls up images of subjugation and even fears of annihilation. Ultimately, in the corner of our minds, we see Hector's mutilated body dragging behind Achilles' chariot. Still more, we see Achilles wielding the power of life and death, dignity and humiliation, and feel ourselves powerless before him.

These overlays of images form the substance of the mystique of dominance, and may serve in the nature of self-fulfilling prophecy. In this context, any defeat may produce a sense of helplessness in the defeated. If the experience of defeat is repeated the feeling of impotence may become overwhelming. One may then observe the conditions which Herbert A. Shepard has described for the "chronically defeated group":

Such a group tends to divide into subgroups and to develop both cliques and social isolates. There is also mutual disparagement among the cliques. Rumor, especially gloomy rumor, is usually abundant. The group itself becomes unattractive to its members. Some members leave, and those who leave are usually considered the "good" ones, leaving those who remain to become even more insecure. The group develops a "servant" self-image; it stops initiating ideas, squashes would-be innovators, and does only what it is sure will be wanted by superiors.

(Shepard, 1964:135)

But this effect may be quite disproportionate to the cause, reflecting a subjective devaluation more than an objective loss of capabilities. Some kinds of defeat do of course involve significant losses of resources and capabilities, but even then it may appear later that the defeated has residual sources of strength, which have been obscured by the mystique of victory.

The moment of victory is a moment of great symbolic impact. But it is a moment, which, having passed, leaves victor and vanquished alike with the problem of defining its meaning. Often this is a process which takes place only over a period of years, sometimes decades or even centuries. In the course of time it often emerges, as Simone Weil observed, that victory "is simply a continual game of seesaw":

The victor of the moment feels himself invincible, even though, only a few hours before, he may have experienced defeat; he forgets to treat victory as a transitory thing.

(Weil, 1956:15)

Thus Germany was victor over France in 1871, defeated in World War I in 1918, swept victorious across the face of Europe in 1939–1942, but was defeated again and reduced to partition in 1945 (nor is it clear that this defeat was final).

Over a somewhat longer time-span, we discern a similar seesaw in China's relations with Western powers. In a classic statement of this relationship, Hosea B. Morse wrote in 1910:

Up to 1839 it was China which dictated to the West the terms on which relations should be permitted to exist: since 1860 it is the West which has imposed on China the conditions of their common intercourse. . . .

(Morse, 1910:299)

But as we know, the down side has swung up again: since 1950, it has again been China which determines the terms on which her relations with the West are permitted to exist.

We have seen that the defeated can be reduced to a thing by annihilation or extermination. We know also that the defeated can be reduced to apathy and enervation by extremes of brutality or exploitation, starvation or dehumanizing treatment. But in their most extreme forms—in the transatlantic slave crossings or the SS extermination camps—these are rare episodes, and even then not without their examples of defiance and rebellion.

Short of such extremes, the defeated is not in fact reduced to a thing, but remains a sentient human person, or an active human group. As such, the *possibility* always remains open to refuse to submit, to reject the will of the victor, to take autonomous action. In practice, the stakes may be too high to act upon this possibility at first, or perhaps indefinitely. On the other hand, it may happen that the "submission" demanded by the victor is relatively so slight that the cost of resistance would not seem worthwhile.

This appears to have been the reasoning of the imperial court of China when it accepted the Treaty of Nanking in 1842. Since that time, the treaty has been heralded in the West as "the opening of China" and "the beginning of the nineteenth-century treaty system in Far Eastern history and of the decline of the Manchu Empire." But to the Manchu court of the time, neither the opening of five treaty ports, the ending of the Cohong monopoly, nor the payment of an indemnity seemed to outweigh the economic and political costs of pursuing seriously a war against the "rebel barbarians" (Teng, 1944:13-14, 145n).

Moreover, neither the imperial court nor the governor-general at Canton, nor the populace of Canton and Kwangtung province, had much intention of fulfilling the terms of the treaty. As Adda Bozeman has pointed out, "Occidental understandings of the meanings of law are not shared by non-Western nations," and in the case of China, "contractual law . . . had no place either in the Legalist or in the Confucian system." In foreign policy, Peking's diplomatic dealings with other peoples "relied heavily on ritual and were always carefully adjusted to the particular susceptibilities of each inferior nation" (Bozeman, 1973:5,15). Thus there was little sense of sacred commitment to treaty obligations on the Chinese side, and as Morse put it, "fourteen years of perpetual friction followed on the peace of 1842" (Morse, 1910:Vol. I, 617). The British in that period were prevented from entering Canton, prevented from communicating directly with the imperial court in Peking, and even obliged in 1849 to accept a revival of the Cohong monopoly (Wakeman, 1966:105).[6]

There followed two more wars, fought in quick succession in 1958–1960, "to settle again the same questions." In the settlement of the second war by the Treaty of Tientsin, according to Morse, "every vestige of Chinese sovereignty was swept away within the limits of the stipulations of the treaties; but the victories of the second war were as inconclusive as those of the first" (Morse, 1910:617). The emperor, having hardly agreed to the terms of the new treaty, decided to have it annulled. Moreover, a party of British and French diplomatic envoys were captured, imprisoned and mistreated in Peking; some twenty of them died or were executed. This led to a renewal of hostilities which, as Morse describes it, finally settled the question of Chinese submission:

This third war, conducted with adequate forces, finally brought China to her knees. . . . now, as the result of three wars, the Chinese learned, and they accepted as their law, that, whereas formerly it was China which dictated the conditions under which international relations were to be maintained, now it was the Western nations which imposed their will on China.

(Morse, 1910:617)

Yet these conclusions of Morse are open to considerable doubt. To begin with, it is unclear that China was "brought to her knees" by Western military force, as much as she was reluctant (as she had been in 1842) and now also less able (because of the Taiping rebellion and other domestic troubles) to throw away resources on a costly war with barbarians over comparatively insignificant stakes. "International relations," understood to mean commerce and diplomatic contact with the West, were altogether much less important matters to the Chinese imperial court in the mid-nineteenth century than they were to eager Western traders and diplomats, or than they seem to us today. To say that China was "brought to her knees" by the war of 1858–1860 is both to exaggerate the extent and reality of the defeat accepted by China, and to deny the rational option of pulling back from a disproportionately costly and destructive war, by confounding that option with the image of submission in general.

Moreover, it is far from clear today what the Western nations gained by "imposing their will on China" in 1860. The myth of the "infinite potentialities" of the China trade soon proved itself illusory:

In spite of continuous efforts on the part of the treaty powers, by armed force and persuasion, to bring China into the international market, the Chinese people showed only passive and slow interest. They had all they wanted of their accustomed daily necessities, such as rice and wheat for food, cotton and silk and fur for clothing, tea and wine for beverage. Moreover, during the early part of that period, the foreign nations had little to offer besides curios like watches and clocks, etc. The nationalist sentiment of the Chinese people, which was opposed to the corrupt and inept Manchu regime and to domination and subjugation by Western powers, as manifest in the Taiping Movement of 1850–64 and the Boxer uprising in 1900, also hampered the development of China's foreign trade during the period under consideration.

(Cheng, 1956:7)

Thus despite the fact that the "open door" was "held open without any protection whatsoever against foreign exploitation or competition," there was hardly any significant increase in the volume of China's total foreign trade between 1860 and 1900. Throughout that period, the trade remained between about $200 and $300 million. After 1900, the expansion of railroad mileage in China led to a rapid increase in the volume of foreign trade by 1913. Even then, however, it was only about $700 million. It rose again during World War I to about $1.8 billion in 1919, which was the high-water mark of the China trade; thereafter, internal civil war and external struggles drove it steadily downward, until in 1936 it was back to the level of 1905: less than $500 million. By comparison, the foreign trade of the United States in 1936 amounted to a total of $5.5 billion, of which only $100 million was with China.[7] This amount was one-fifth of China's total trade, but only one fifty-fifth of U.S. trade. Forty-five years later, and over a century after the Peking conventions of 1860, the China door is almost completely closed.

John Fairbanks has argued that what the Western-dominated treaty system did in China was to make representatives of the Western powers partners in "a Sino-Western rule over China, which by degrees came to supplant the Manchu-Chinese synarchy of the Ch'ing period" (Fairbanks, 1953:467). This phenomenon had a variety of precedents in Chinese history, above all in the fact that "barbarian invaders of China had often acquired the dominant power in the Confucian state without destroying its political structure" (Fairbanks, 1953:465). But while this was nice for the ego of the Western partners, and useful to the Manchus in prolonging their rule, and profitable to some financial and trading interests, and perhaps influential in Chinese society in ways which still remain to be investigated, it is extremely doubtful that it meant that Western nations could "impose their will on China" in any general sense.

Evidently, they could not coerce China into buying or selling more than she could or would, given the cultural tastes and economic conditions of her population. Nor could they remake China in their own image, as they might have hoped to do, for neither the imperial regime in the late nineteenth century nor the Republican government after 1911 had the power to control or even to set the direction of Chinese political and social life. China simply had no effective central government for most of the period of Western intervention. Though this contributed to the freedom of action of Westerners on Chinese territory, it also limited severely the significance of "Sino-Western rule." Throughout the period, it was primarily Chinese rebels or warlords, militia or intellectuals, gentry or peasants, bourgeois or workers, who shaped the life and the future of the country. By comparison with these, the Manchu-Chinese-Western synarchy of the era after 1860 reminds us of Malthus's remark that "institutions are a feather" (Malthus, 1959).[8]

It seems clear then, that to characterize the defeat of China in the Opium Wars of the mid-nineteenth century as having brought her "to her knees" or imposed upon her an absolute submission to the will of the Western powers is at best inaccurate and simplistic, at worst misleading in a way which reinforces the mystique of dominance. The concessions granted were limited, less significant at the outset in Chinese than in Western eyes, and ultimately of dubious value—or perhaps directly counterproductive to Western interests and influence in China.

But what of the harsher case in which the defeated are indeed directly subjugated to foreign rule, particularly for a prolonged period and with severely exploitative treatment? The history of European and American imperialism makes clear that this can result in the destruction of millions and tens of millions of human lives. The Congo under Belgian rule is reported to have been reduced from a population variously estimated as between twenty and forty million at the time of conquest to a population of barely over eight million in 1926 (Moon, 1926:95). This took place through overwork, brutality, famine, executions, suppression of rebellion, flight, and disruption of the native culture and economy. This spectacular toll of lives, however, was less usual than the reduction of the colonized people to the pattern of the "chronically defeated group," for example as described by Frantz Fanon:

The town belonging to the colonized people, or at least the native town, the Negro village, the medina, the reservation, is a place of ill fame, peopled by men of evil repute. They are born there, it matters not where, nor how. It is a world without spaciousness; men live there on top of each other, and their huts are built one on top of the other. The native town is a hungry town, starved of bread, of meat, of shoes, of coal, of light. The native town is a crouching village, a town on its knees, a town wallowing in the mire.

(Fanon, 1968:39)

Yet Fanon also sets the counterpoint to the image of defeat as permanent subjugation, submission, or impotence. For he sees that the posture of submission may become—indeed perhaps must become—a mask.

Confronted with a world ruled by the settler, the native is always presumed guilty. But the native's guilt is never a guilt which he accepts; it is rather a kind of curse, a sort of sword of Damocles, for, in his innermost spirit, the native admits no accusation. He is dominated but not domesticated; he is treated as an inferior but he is not convinced of his inferiority. He is patiently waiting until the settler is off his guard to fly at him. The native's muscles are always tensed.[9]

(Fanon, 1968:53)

The passage from submission to rebellion is, from Fanon's viewpoint, the inevitable consequence of the pattern of subjugation itself. However separate the settler's town may be from the native town, however Manichaean the colonial world may be, the settler's life is always in view, and the native is always confronted with the naked force which maintains its well-lit, well-fed air. "The look that the native turns on the settler's town is a look of lust, a look of envy;—it expresses his dreams of possession—all manner of possession: to sit at the settler's table, to sleep in the settler's bed, with his wife if possible." Moreover, the colonizers hardly bother to conceal the coercion on which their rule is based. Whereas in the imperialist home countries a host of moralizers, educators and traditions cloak the dominance of the rulers in legitimacy, in the colonies

. . . the policeman and the soldier, by their immediate presence and their frequent and direct action maintain contact with the native and advise him by means of rifle butts and napalm not to budge. It is obvious here that the agents of government speak the language of pure force. The inter-mediary does not lighten the oppression, nor seek to hide the domination; he shows them up and puts them into practice with the clear conscience of an upholder of the peace; yet he is the bringer of violence into the home and into the mind of the native.

(Fanon, 1968:38)

Finally, in the Manichaean world of the colonists, the natives must be reduced to animals. But this also feeds the springs of rebellion. The native

. . . laughs to himself every time he spots an allusion to the animal world in the other's words. For he knows that he is not an animal; and it is precisely at the moment that he realizes his humanity that he begins to sharpen the weapons with which he will secure its victory.

(Fanon, 1968:43)

In Algeria, the victory of the native rebellion against French rule was won, though only after prolonged struggle. In other places, such as South Africa, the struggle is still in process, its outcome uncertain.

In some cases, however, the limitations on a conqueror's ability to control and exploit a subject population appear much more rapidly. Thus Germany during World War II was able to exploit the French economy to such an extent that by the fall of 1943 some 40 to 50 percent of France's industrial production was for German purposes; yet efforts to impose labor conscription upon French workers for labor service in Germany proved a failure within a few months. At the outset, French workers went to work in Germany voluntarily in considerable numbers, out of a combi-nation of incentives and pressures; and the first months of the labor con-scription (May-July 1943) were also moderately successful, so that in the autumn of 1943, French workers composed the largest ethnic group in the foreign labor force in Germany (26.3 percent of the foreign male workers).

But resistance to labor conscription mounted rapidly, with doubly negative effects for Germany. Departures of French workers for Germany fell by August 1943 to their lowest level since the summer of 1942, and became statistically insignificant thereafter (Milward, 1970:112–113-123-124 *et passim*). At the same time, the labor conscription drove thousands of French men into the Resistance. In any case, German exploitation of the economy of France was plagued with inescapable contradictions. While occupation payments, looting, and other direct exactions weakened the capacity of French industry to produce for German war purposes, labor productivity was also reduced sharply by worsened conditions and passive resistance or active sabotage. Inflation and the black market further reflected the limits on German ability to control the French economy, as well as increasing the difficulties of exploiting it. As Alan Milward concluded:

It is the behavior of the French labour force during the war, and, indeed, the whole history of the French resistance movement, which assert that the economics of conquest cannot wholly be calculated in terms of cash.
(Milward, 1970:288)

The Germans also found themselves unable to impose certain other policies on the French when the population chose to resist: for example, efforts to destroy the Jewish population of France met with such widespread resistance that some three-fourths of the Jews were saved, whereas in other countries, especially in eastern Europe, the Jewish populations were almost exterminated. Raul Hilberg attributes this in part to the Germans' need for French assistance in carrying out deportations: "In no territory . . . was German dependence upon native administration so great as in France. . . . Because of the increasing French reluctance to cooperate in arrests and seizures, the German police were gradually forced to rely upon their own resources. . . . While the Germans thus stepped into the open, the Jews, with the aid of the French organizations, began to submerge. The prospective victims went into hiding by the tens of thousands, and, wherever possible, they moved across the borders" (Hilberg, 1961:389–418).

That the breadth and effectiveness of French resistance to exploitation and genocide was more the exception than the rule in Europe under Hitler is not to be denied. Nevertheless, it makes clear that the consequences of victory are not self-defined, nor defined by the victor independent of the defeated. What made defeated France more resistant than, say, defeated

Poland cannot be examined here, but we would suggest that the answer lies more in the conditions and values to which the defeated populations were accustomed than in differences in policy adopted by the victorious Germans. We need to look more closely than we have yet done at the defeated, if we hope to arrive at an adequate answer to this question.

That experience of self-realization, of assertion of one's own humanity, which Fanon saw as a prelude to the victory of rebellion, may lead at first to the extinction of the individual person. This was the case for Private Eddie Slovik, the sole U.S. soldier to be shot for desertion in World War II, and indeed the only one to be executed for desertion since the Civil War. Slovik was almost unknown when he died and has been quite forgotten in the past decade, despite the national debate about desertion from the armed forces occasioned by the war in Vietnam.[10] But Slovik is one of those rare cases of the utterly powerless, chronically defeated persons whose fate has been documented because he was singled out for the final defeat—annihilation—to serve as a warning to his fellows (Huie, 1954). A warning of what? That remains one of the key questions of his case.

On January 31, 1945, the day Eddie Slovik was executed, he said to an MP sergeant: "They're not shooting me for deserting the United States Army—thousands of guys have done that. They're shooting me for bread I stole when I was twelve years old." This makes him sound a little like a left-wing ideologue, but he was nothing of the kind. He was a "dead-end kid," a depression boy from Hamtramck and Detroit, who called himself "just a dum Polack" and had a record of arrests for petty thievery. He had spent two stretches of time in the Michigan Reformatory at Ionia, but prison was not a school of revolution for Slovik. Slovik was never a rebel and never inclined to violence. On the contrary, he was highly conformist and not a hater. Harry Dimmick, the supervisor at the reformatory, who had taken Eddie under his wing, remembered him as "a friendly, good-hearted kid." His army buddies remembered him as doing favors for everybody: "Best-hearted guy I ever met. Everybody liked him." One told William Bradford Huie, Slovik's biographer: "Eddie just didn't hate anybody, not even Germans" (Huie, 1954:24).

Slovik didn't hate people, but he hated guns. This was not a matter of ideology, but of gut reaction. Dimmick described Slovik as insecure and fearful, "a lone wolf . . . never laughed much, or played jokes. . . but he never had a fight while he was here . . . never made an enemy.

Weak as dishwater, sure, scared, insecure. . . . Eddie was weak and soft, scared but gentle" (Huie, 1954:24).

While in training, Slovik wrote his wife repeatedly that he hated to shoot, hated his rifle. His scores were very low, partly because of ineptness, partly because he hoped the army would discharge him: "I am going on the rifle range Sat. and I am going to foul up. I'll try to have a poor score so they won't send me overseas. If I am dum on everything they might send me home cause I won't be able to fight." The army wanted him to wear glasses, but he refused. Whether deliberately or not, he did very poorly with a rifle. "I couldn't even hit the darn dummy." He did somewhat better with a machine gun, and wrote Antoinette: "I had a pretty good score. But I hate guns." Sometime before he was sent into combat, Slovik decided he would never use his rifle. On the ship in which he crossed the Atlantic in August 1944, he told a buddy: "I don't know why the hell I'm cleaning this rifle. I never intend to fire it" (Huie, 1954: 72, 82, 83, 112).

Slovik hated the army, which he found even worse than his prison experiences. He saw it as an anonymous collective body—"they"—which was trying to destroy the short-lived happiness he had finally found, for less than two years of his life, just before he was drafted. He wrote Antoinette: ". . . ever since I was born I've had hard luck. I spent five years in jail, got out when I was 22, got married when I was 22, lived 15 months with my darling wife and was so happy with her, and now they break up my happiness, put me in the army, and try to kill us both and take everything we've got" (Huie, 1954:99–100).

The notion that the army was trying to kill them both was by no means sheer paranoia. Like Yossarian in Heller's *Catch-22*, Slovik had come to the clear recognition that, by sending him into combat, "they" were trying to kill him. Whether they *wanted* to kill him was irrelevant to the fact that bodies were needed to kill and be killed, and that he was to be one of those bodies. As for Antoinette, she had had a miscarriage and a series of epileptic seizures after Slovik was drafted, had been unable to work, barely able to care for herself, and unsuccessful in getting any assistance from the Red Cross. That "they" were trying to kill both Eddie and Antoinette Slovik was therefore not so far-fetched as it sounded.

Nevertheless, Eddie Slovik did not go overseas with either a pacifist ideology or a plan to desert. What happened was that he found himself one day in a foxhole, under fire, and simply stayed there when the rest of his group moved on. Thereafter he spent some time with Canadian troops, and was finally returned to his own unit. In his confession he recorded:

I told my commanding officer my story. I said that if I had to go out their again I'd run away. He said their was nothing he could do for me so I ran away again AND I'LL RUN AWAY AGAIN IF I HAVE TO GO OUT THEIR (Huie, 1954:142–143).

Slovik believed that they had chosen to execute him, of all the deserters who had been caught but had been sentenced to lighter punishments, because of his civilian record, beginning with thefts of bread and cake when he was twelve. And it does appear from the remarks of military personnel involved in the case that they were somewhat influenced by Slovik's record. General McNeil, for example, wrote explicitly that "His unfavorable civilian record indicates that he is not a worthy subject of clemency." And the Staff Judge Advocate's review argued that his prior offenses, though "not of sufficient gravity to influence my recommendation," did

indicate a persistent refusal to conform to the rules of society in civilian life, an imperviousness to penal correction and a total lack of appreciation of clemency. . . .

(Huie, 1954:188)

On the contrary, both Slovik's offenses and his later behavior indicated a high degree of conformity to the rules of whichever society Slovik found himself in: at first, the street culture of his adolescence; later, the reformatory at Ionia; briefly, a good job and his marriage in Dearborn; finally, the society of his buddies in the army. Everywhere he showed himself a good worker, eager to please, helpful to all, serious, trustworthy, sincere. But at the point at which "they" not only came between him and his brief rendezvous with happiness, at that point at which they demanded that Eddie Slovik should kill and be killed, he refused.

As the Judge Advocate's review makes plain, this was indeed the unpardonable heart of Slovik's crime against the United States of America:

He was *obstinately determined not to engage in combat*, and on two occasions, the second after express warning as to results, he deserted. He *boldly confessed* to these offenses and concluded his confession with the statement, "so I ran away again AND I'LL RUN AWAY AGAIN IF I

HAVE TO GO OUT THEIR." There can be no doubt that he deliberately sought *the safety and comparative comfort* of the guardhouse. To him and to those soldiers who may follow his example, if he achieves his end, confinement is neither deterrent nor punishment. He has *directly challenged the authority of the government*, and *future discipline depends* upon a resolute reply to this challenge.

(Huie, 1954; italics added)

However, even this statement does not go deeply enough into the reasons why Eddie Slovik had to be annihilated, rather than punished with some lesser penalty, nor why future discipline was seen to depend so much on the response to this particular deserter. Conscientious objectors, draft dodgers, malingerers, and even other deserters, had shown themselves "obstinately determined not to engage in combat," had sought "the safety and comparative comfort" of prisons and guardhouses in order to escape it, and in some cases had also "directly challenged the authority of the government," without being condemned to execution. What was it, then, about Slovik's case that so frightened and enraged his military judges?

No one can be certain of this today, but I would suggest that it was Slovik's symbolic universality rather than his uniqueness which brought him before the firing squad. Had his desertion been the consequence of middle-class pacifist conviction or conversion, he would have seemed less threatening because pacifist ideology still had very limited appeal at that time, and perhaps also because the judges would have had more empathy with one of their own kind, by class if not by outlook. On the other hand, had he cloaked his desertion in excuses or other placatory rituals, he would have seemed less threatening because, in conforming to expected lowerclass behavior, he would not have approached as close as he did to exposing the profound insecurity of the "authority of the government" and of "future discipline." On the face of it, in fact, it would seem ludicrous that Eddie Slovik, the dead-end kid, the scared semi-literate nobody, totally lacking in any of the skills, resources, connections, or perquisites which we associate with power, could have been seen as a serious threat to phenomena so august and sweeping as the "authority of the government" and the future discipline of its armed forces. But it was precisely because of what he was, and because he openly attributed his desertion to basic human emotions of fear and self-preservation rather than to ideology or error, that the threat he posed was so real and profound. If Slovik could refuse to fight and thereby save himself, so might indeed *any* other soldier.

For Slovik was far from unique, or even unusual, in his revulsion against the use of guns in combat, particularly against the use of rifles in direct personal combat. S. L. A. Marshall and others who studied the behavior of infantrymen in Europe and the Pacific in World War II found that "not more than 15 percent of the men had actually fired at the enemy positions or personnel with rifles, carbines, grenades, bazookas, BARs or machine guns during the course of an entire engagement" (Marshall, 1947:50, 54–57). Moreover, those who did fire were generally the same men, in engagement after engagement, and generally "heavy weapons men"—those firing automatic rifles, flamethrowers and bazookas, and those back of the lines in artillery crews. "Thus the ordinary rifleman was found to fire his rifle very infrequently in any given engagement of World War II" (Prosterman, 1972:103).

What was unusual about Slovik, therefore, was that he declared openly his intention not to fire his rifle, on the basis of simple feelings of fear and disgust, rather than following the advice of a buddy who had warned him that he could "get into trouble for saying things like that." What this soldier and some 85 percent of his fellows dimly realized was that they could get into *more* trouble by *saying* "things like that" than by doing them. Clearly neither training, nor exhortations, nor the actual experience of being under fire could persuade or coerce the vast majority of infantry soldiers to shoot at "the enemy" in combat; but they knew better than to avow this openly. Slovik paid with his life for that avowal.

Again, one can only speculate as to why it was perceived as so dangerous or intolerable that Slovik had to die for it. But it seems not too far-fetched to suggest that what Slovik threatened was the *mystique* of dominance. For the dominant to preserve their position, the *appearance* of command and obedience must be maintained, even if the reality has a hollow core. For the supposedly powerless to express their real power by surreptitious inaction on the battlefield, could be overlooked because the magnitude and meaning of this noncompliance with the will of the dominant remained (and remains) unknown and ambiguous. But for Eddie Slovik, the most powerless of the powerless, to refuse compliance openly and entirely on his own initiative, without reference to ideology, organizational supports, or "outside agitators," was indeed a profound threat to "the authority of government."

To literary and patriotic elites, it may seem blasphemous to compare Slovik and Hector, far removed as they were by class, culture, values, and actions. On the other hand, some of us may find the comparison un-favorable to Hector, who emerges from the *Iliad* a mindless battle-glutton, with few traits we would care to emulate today. For our purposes here, however, we note that Slovik shared with Hector this aspect of the fate of the defeated: he could not simply be eliminated. He had to live again after his death, else the victory over him would have been meaningless. His execution was announced widely, if laconically, to American troops still in service in the last months of World War II, expressly to warn them against desertion, which was on the increase at the time. Thereafter, it seemed that the Army had forgotten Slovik. Nonetheless, the full coopera-tion offered by Army officials and military personnel in providing William Bradford Huie with materials for his book on Slovik suggests that they saw no reason to suppress his memory. On the contrary, they probably welcomed the opportunity to justify themselves and confirm the meaning of Slovik's defeat, as they saw it, and of their victory over him.

As we have seen, however, victory is a seesaw. We know more about Slovik today than we do about most of his fellows precisely because he was singled out for extinction. And in his letters, in the documents and reminiscenes of his case, we may discover meanings which point towards the defeat of his victors.

Yet the recognition that victory is a seesaw leaves too much unsaid. It leaves a host of attendant questions which have hardly been touched: for example, what accounts for the duration of the swings? Does the game sometimes end—(and if so, when or how?)—as it seems to have done for the ancient societies of the Near East and the classical world? Or are those also instances of the cultural conquest of the victors by the defeated, as Greece is said to have conquered Rome? Are there some chronically defeated groups or nations which have been driven out of the game al-together, or never entered it? Or is the absence of such groups—e.g., women—from the seesaw an illusion, based on false conceptions of the nature of power and victory?

In any case, the assertion that victory is a seesaw leaves unexamined the processes by which the defeated is transformed into the victor. More fundamental still, it leaves unchallenged the mystique of dominance which attaches to the notion of victory. These points are not unrelated. For the process by which the seesaw changes the direction of its swing could never take place if the mystique of dominance were sound. If indeed victory is attended by domination, and domination implies control and sub-jugation, if indeed the defeated is constrained by the victor to accept submission and impotence, how can the defeated reverse the direction of the swing?

Sometimes the answer given to this question is: the defeated cannot; the reversal takes place only through a weakening or corruption of the victor, or through outside intervention, or through the emergence of a "new class" with suitable economic or intellectual resources for "leadership." But this is too ready an answer, and too self-serving for dominant or would-be elites. It preserves intact the mystique of dominance, insisting in effect that the powerless—the nondominant, the nonelite, the poor, the unorganized or uneducated—are indeed submissive and impotent and must forever remain so until touched by the awakening kiss of Prince Charming (or Chairman Mao?).

It may be that this position will someday be proved beyond doubt; that the effort to find a foreign or middle-class or intellectual *deus ex machina* (always of the male sex) to explain every popular movement, or at least, every successful popular movement in history will ultimately be rewarded, and the high priests of the cult of power will be able to sleep easy, secure in the knowledge that the masses remain inert.

But reason and evidence are both available to suggest another view. The evidence is still scant and obscure, but if we seek further in the direction it points, we may find ourselves able to confirm that dominance itself is never complete, that it is always at least partially a myth. The defeat of a particular insurgent group may be followed by the success of its objectives not long afterward; the concessions granted by a defeated nation may be withdrawn or may prove to be empty shells in later decades; the exploitation of a subject population will prove to have internal contradictions and limits set by the residual powers of the defeated; even the victory which seems most complete, the annihilation of the defeated, often requires that the victim be resurrected, with consequences which the victor may be unable to control. The powers which the defeated retain are difficult to assess because they are heavily obscured by the mystique of victory. They are the "powers of the powerless," which I have discussed elsewhere (Carroll, 1972:607–614), and often also many powers conventionally ascribed to the powerful. For while the powerless—those lacking the power of dominance—are far from impotent, the defeated are in many cases not even "powerless" in the conventional meaning of the term.

Thus victory can never in itself secure the "fruits of victory." These depend on the defeated, with whom the victor stands in a symbiotic relationship, whose character is still not well understood. In order to understand it, we need to look less in the direction of victory and dominance, where the mystique tends to overwhelm the reality, and examine more closely the nature of defeat and submission, which are more complex and multidimensional than is generally recognized. It may be that when we do this, we will find that to challenge the *appearance* of victory and dominance is to forge an instrument for their defeat. Perhaps it will then emerge that we need not play that desperate game of seesaw eternally, that there are other—more real and fundamental—bases of human interaction than victory and defeat, dominance and submission. Perhaps those who have been off the seesaw longest, namely women, have most to contribute to that.

NOTES

1. Simone Weil calls attention to these or similar scenes in the *Iliad*, though her quotations do not coincide exactly with those used here.

2. See the *Journal of Peace Research*, special issue on peace research in history, December 1969, especially: Raymond G. O'Connor, "Victory in Modern War," and B. A. Carroll, "How Wars End: An Analysis of Some Current Hypotheses."

3. As explicitly noted by the authors, the determinations of "victor" and "defeated" nations were not based on "operational indicators," but on "consensus among acknowledged specialists." In personal conversation, Singer has explained that the determinations were made at a brainstorming session early in the work of the "Correlates of War" project; i.e., the "consensus among acknowledged specialists" was the consensus of the project's research staff and other well-known social scientists present at that time.

4. See Calahan, 1944. For discussion, see Carroll, 1969.

5. I am indebted to Clinton F. Fink for calling Timasheff's work to my attention, and for other references and discussions of points treated in this paper.

6. Wakeman often seems in this book to be arguing a position contrary to the underlying viewpoint of this paper; for example, he is at pains to argue that "gentry leadership, not peasant spontaneity, was the essential factor" behind the San-yuan-li incident, allegedly a great popular victory of peasant troops over a British attacking force (Wakeman, 1966:14–40). On the other hand, much of the substance of Wakeman's material seems to point in a different direction, which he himself makes explicit in the introduction: "In short, underneath that overlying surface of official history, there burgeoned mass fears, mass hopes, mass movements" (Wakeman, 1966:6).

7. Figures on China's trade from Cheng, 1956:258–259; figures on United States trade from Enyclopedia Britannica, article on International Trade.

8. I am indebted to Kenneth Boulding for calling this to my attention.

9. I have substituted "dominated but not domesticated" in place of "overpowered but not tamed" in translation of the original phrase: "dominé mais non domestiqué."

10. Since this was first written in 1973, a television documentary and the efforts of Antoinette Slovik have recalled Slovik to public attention.

REFERENCES

Bozeman, Adda. "Law and Foreign Policy: Problems in Intercultural Communication." Paper read at the annual meeting of the International Studies Association, New York, March 1973, mimeo.

Calahan, H. A., *What Makes a War End?* New York, 1944.

Carroll, Berenice A. "Peace Research: The Cult of Power." *Journal of Conflict Resolution*, 1972, *16*, 585–616.

Carroll, Berenice A. "How Wars End: An Analysis of Some Current Hypotheses." *Journal of Peace Research*, December 1969, pp. 295–320.

Cheng, Yu-Kwei. *Foreign Trade and Industrial Development of China.* Washington, D.C.: University Press of Washington, 1956.

Fairbanks, John K. *Trade and Diplomacy on the China Coast, 1842-1854*, vol. 1. Cambridge, Mass.: Harvard University Press, 1953.

Fanon, Frantz. *The Wretched of the Earth.* New York: Grove Press, 1968.

Hilberg, Raul. *The Destruction of the European Jews.* Chicago: Quadrangle Books, 1961.

Homer. *The Iliad of Homer.* (Ennis Rees, trans.) New York: Random House (Modern Library), 1963.

Huie, William Bradford. *The Execution of Private Slovik.* New York: Duell, Sloan and Pearce, 1954.

Malthus, Thomas. *Population: The First Essay.* Ann Arbor: University of Michigan Press, 1959.

Marshall, S. L. A. *Men Against Fire.* New York: William Morrow, 1947.

Milward, Alan S. *The New Order and the French Economy.* London: Oxford University Press, 1970.

Modelski, George. "International Settlement of Internal War." In James N. Rosenau (ed.), *International Aspects of Civil Strife.* Princeton: Princeton University Press, 1964.

Moon, Parker T. *Imperialism and World Politics.* New York: Macmillan, 1926.

Morse, Hosea B. *International Relations of the Chinese Empire.* London: Longmans, Green, 1910.

O'Connor, Raymond G. "Victory in Modern War." *Journal of Peace Research*, December 1969, pp. 367–380.

Prosterman, Roy L. *Surviving to 3000: An Introduction to the Study of Lethal Conflict.* Belmont, California: Duxbury Press (Wadsworth), 1972.

Randle, Robert F. *The Origins of Peace.* New York: The Free Press, 1973.

Shepard, Herbert A. "Responses to Situations of Competition and Conflict." In Robert L. Kahn and Elise Boulding (eds.), *Power and Conflict in Organizations.* New York: Basic Books, 1964.

Singer, J. David and Small, Melvin. *The Wages of War: 1816-1965: A Statistical Handbook.* New York: Wiley, 1972.

Teng, Ssu-yu. *Chang-Hsi and the Treaty of Nanking, 1842.* Chicago: University of Chicago Press, 1944.

Timasheff, Nicholas S. *War and Revolution.* New York: Sheed and Ward, 1965.

Wakeman, Frederic, Jr. Strangers at the Gate: *Social Disorder in South China, 1839-1861.* Berkeley: University of California Press, 1966.

Weil, Simone. *The Iliad, or The Poem of Force.* Wallingford, Pa.: Pendle Hill, 1956.

JAY L. KAPLAN

4
VICTORY AND VANQUISHED:
Their Postwar Relations

POSTWAR COERCION AND THE UTILITY
OF TOTAL CONVENTIONAL WARFARE

Modern warfare between major states has been characterized by an expansion of both the means to inflict violence and the political objectives of the combatants. It also has been characterized by diminished utility, as the expanded means of pursuing military victory have paradoxically failed to secure the expanded objectives victory is now expected to serve. Part I of this essay explores this contradiction. The analysis concentrates upon the difficulties in attaining more than minimal defensive goals, even in the wake of conclusive victory in a total conventional war,[1] especially one in which the winning side is composed of a coalition of states.

The aftermath of World War I provides the clearest illustration of the bankruptcy of such a victory. Germany's defeat permitted the victors to do what they pleased to the enemy population, but only in terms of the infliction of misery. Not only did coercion carry high costs for the Allies, it failed to achieve its basic purposes and contributed to the renewal of war in 1939. The analysis of Part I is applied to a case study of the years following World War I in Part II of this essay.

In his famous assertion that "war is only a part of political intercourse, therefore by no means an independent thing in itself,"[2] Karl von Clausewitz provided a prescription for maximizing the instrumental functions of force. Success in war, as in any means-ends relationship, depends upon the effectiveness of the means employed and their appropriateness and economy in relation to the ends pursued. The effectiveness of force is a function of its sufficiency and the relative skill with which it is employed. Its appropriateness is determined by its fungibility: the military objectives secured by force are proximate ends whose value is determined by their convertibility into political benefits. The economy of war can be expressed as the sum of these benefits minus the costs of force.[3] The costliness of military effectiveness in total conventional warfare is inherently prejudicial to a favorable balance. Only if vast political benefits are derived from military victory will the outcome be positive. But while firepower and its associated costs have expanded drastically since the time of von Clausewitz, the conversion value of military victory has remained relatively static. Military victory in total conventional war is still most appropriate to the achievement of modest political objectives.

The expansion of the means and ends of war has contributed to situations where war does indeed become "an independent thing in itself." The "expansion of force"[4] has placed in the hands of statesmen bludgeons that are ill suited to delicate discrimination among political objectives. Furthermore, escalation in war tends to follow its own logic and momentum, as each state feels compelled to respond to the most aggressive interpretation of the intentions underlying its enemy's behavior. When core values including national political survival are perceived to be threatened, there is a temptation to use all available force to escalate or prolong the struggle rather than concede defeat. This initiates a vicious circle. For, as the costs of conflict climb, there is a tendency for victory programs to expand beyond the original war objectives in order to justify and give meaning to losses already suffered as well as to maintain domestic support for the war. But as victory becomes more retributive, defeat becomes more catastrophic, serving as a grim incentive to greater violence. The costs of this irrational momentum of decisions—each of which might well demonstrate a "limited rationality" when viewed as an incremental problem of value maximization—may easily outstrip the benefits. For while costs tend to spiral upward, the values secured by increased violence do not generally rise proportionately. In some instances, in fact, they may actually diminish.

Values or benefits may be measured in terms of the achievement of the defensive and offensive goals of war. Defensive goals relate to the narrowly conceived identity, integrity, and security of the antagonists. Offensive goals concern values which a contestant would seek to impose upon or extract from the vanquished enemy and the international environment. For reasons which will be explored below, defensive goals may be achieved more economically than offensive goals in total conventional wars. Even with respect to defensive goals, however, the process of escalation or prolongation of violence not only imperils the survival of large segments of the opposing populations, but the identity of the rival polities, societies, and economies is altered by the strain of the very attempts at preservation. For the victors, the domestic conflict which might result from such strain can obstruct the postwar policies necessary to the attainment of offensive goals. Conversely, the destruction caused to the enemy often is counterproductive in terms of offensive goals, with the spoils of victory turned to ashes. Furthermore, the wartime costs incurred in the pursuit of offensive goals are only partial. By their nature, such goals are far more difficult to realize than narrower aims. They entail persistently high costs of enforcement well into the postwar period. Finally, frustrations in attaining offensive goals after the war may well aggravate divisions within and among the victor states.

The balance of costs and benefits will tend to be more favorable in situations where the opponents are unequally armed, motivated, and skilled or where their political programs are more limited. Guerrilla wars, civil wars, limited wars, wars fought on another nation's territory, and wars between states of unequal technological capacity can yield net benefits to the stronger or more skillful party. These are all situations where the costs to at least one party can be kept low relative to the values at stake at the outset of the conflict. Of course, in guerrilla or civil wars, and in certain wars between unequals (which can be fought as a limited war by at least one party), this is frequently due to the inestimable value of what is at stake: an entire way of life, life itself, in fact, for those associated with the causes of the combatants. On the other hand, it is important to emphasize that this does not mean that such wars necessarily pay. Even for the stronger party, the costs might escalate to an intolerable level in relation to the value of the objectives. One important distinction, however, can be drawn between these forms of warfare and strategic nuclear or total conventional war. In the former cases, unlike the latter, the tendency toward a lack of utility, measured in terms of offensive goals, is not an inherent characteristic.[5]

THE ENFORCEMENT OF ALLIED VICTORY PROGRAMS

Expanding upon a point made by Georg Simmel, Lewis Coser has written:

Antagonism against a common enemy may be a binding element in two ways. It may either lead to the formation of new groups with distinct boundary lines, ideologies, loyalties and common values, or, stopping short of this, may result only in instrumental associations in the face of a common threat. The emergence of such associations of otherwise isolated individuals represents a "minimum" of unification.[6]

Total warfare may be regarded as the ultimate form of antagonism and polarization in international politics. It imposes the unitary imperative of victory or, at least, survival upon national policy. For two or more nations whose core values appear to be threatened by a common enemy, the primacy of self-preservation may provide the impetus for the minimal type of instrumental association described by Coser.

The cohesion imposed on nations and alliances by the self-evident priority of survival is usually a prerequisite to the achievement of offensive goals. In fact, serious threats to survival tend to generate such goals. More precisely, pressures for the enlargement of the victory program are frequently a function of the magnitude of suffering which a nation or alliance undergoes, one indicator of which is the extent to which threats to security values force sacrifices in welfare values.[7] The greater the deprivation, as a rule, the greater will be the pressures for an expansive victory program. But since the impact of war upon those engaged in fighting or home-front activities is differential, these pressures for satisfaction, compensation, or retribution are diverse, divergent, or contradictory. The expectations aroused by victory on the part of domestic groups and individuals result in a proliferation of competing projects. Whereas war dictates the primacy of security values, in peacetime these must compete with welfare values, just as welfare values compete with one another. Freed from wartime constraints, the decision-making process becomes relatively more pluralistic, and priorities tend to fluctuate with the political fortunes of their advocates.

The incoherence of the postwar program is multiplied in the case of an allied victory. When the minimal and instrumental purposes for which a coalition was formed have been realized, the coalition loses its *raison d'être*. This is true, of course, unless the association has been cemented by unity on broader purposes. In the immediate postwar period it is likely that in certain areas harmony will prevail, while in others the situation will be one of dissension. The mixture of discord and cooperation will fall somewhere along a functional continuum. It is as possible for an alliance to continue in name with little real content as it is to imagine an end to formal ties followed by extensive cooperation. It can be anticipated that the areas of greatest cooperation will be those deriving from the nature and purpose of the alliance itself, the defensive goals that are the common root of interdependence in high politics, diplomacy, and strategy. Cultural, social, economic, and ideological values, stemming as they do from the distinctive national situations of the individual allies, are far more likely to be areas where cooperation will be more difficult. Unfortunately, they also tend to be the areas of greatest concern to the domestic constituency of each unit of the victorious coalition.

Another irony of the conflict between strategy and the extraction or imposition of values in a total war situation is the product of the rational military dictum of "divide and conquer." Both during war and following victory, the fragmentation of an opposing coalition and the isolation of its member units is necessary for the achievement of maximum coercion, a situation where each member of the defeated alliance is confronted with the combined weight of its adversaries. After overt hostilities are terminated, the possibility of the enemy's resurgence remains a binding force upon the successful alliance. But the plurality of other goals within each of the units and between them creates disintegrative tensions. The demands made of the defeated state will tend to reinforce its will to resist, while competition among the victors will provide it with the means to play them off, one against the other.[8] In turn, of course, the victorious coalition can attempt to foster disunity in the vanquished state, but only at the risk of undermining the reestablished political structure it seeks to employ as its agent.

It is clear that the nature of the allied victory shapes the postwar capabilities of the alliance to exploit its success. Total victory, the obverse of unconditional surrender, leaves the enemy completely at the mercy of the opposing armies, incapable of mounting significant armed resistance. In this circumstance, the allies are free to impose whatever conditions they choose upon the vanquished state. Many of these decisions, especially those which are most clearly political in nature, require no act of compliance or cooperation on the part of the defeated state. The redrawing of formal political boundaries is an example of an action susceptible to execution by superior force. Other types of decisions, particularly those in the realm of social, economic, and ideological changes which the victors seek to impose upon the society of the vanquished are of a different nature, requiring, as they do, cooperative actions on the part of the defeated population. These decisions are not self-executing; they cannot be effected by the authority of military dictates. They depend, instead, upon modification of the normal behavioral patterns of the subject population. Some of the difficulties involved, especially for an allied coalition, in employing military force for this purpose include: achieving agreement among the allies on the importance of the objective; deciding upon the nature of the threat; transmitting the threat effectively; absorbing and dividing the high costs of this course of action.

Naturally, all of these elements are cast into a different light depending upon whether or not the victors have chosen to occupy the enemy's territory. With forces in place, they are in a better position to choose their targets, to tailor their methods of coercion in an appropriate manner, and to apply coercion with greater precision. When threats fail, they are in a position either physically to force compliance with demands or actually to employ their troops to execute the orders, all at far less incremental cost than if the troops were stationed outside the defeated state. The drawback, of course, lies in the enormous expenses involved in maintaining an army of occupation. These are both of a material and moral order. Furthermore, the humiliation of foreign occupation can entail the long-run problem of heightened sentiments of revenge. This is particularly the case if the occupation army has been perceived as brutal and repressive, which is likely in proportion to its success in extracting local, and imposing foreign, values.[9]

Limited victory, corresponding to the enemy's conditional surrender, naturally places greater obstacles in the way of controlling the administration of the allied program for the defeated state. In some senses, of course, any victory that does not result in the dissolution of the enemy state and its replacement by a totally new state or its incorporation into an existing state is in some degree limited, for it is an implicit recognition of the residual authority of indigenous political expressions, of the costs in overcoming local loyalties, and of the potential utility to the victor of existing structures and attitudes. Obviously, the nature of the obstacles this creates is a function of the concessions and the effective means available to the vanquished for securing observance of the agreed regime. In certain respects, however, the advantages of a war concluded on such terms do not accrue unilaterally to the defeated state. Insofar as the need to negotiate with the enemy was obvious, domestic forces within the victorious coalition, as well as within the defeated state, are likely to be forced to moderate their pressures, strengthening the hands of their leaders. Furthermore, explicitly negotiated end games which erect a structure of mutual responsibilities and benefits are less likely than a victor's peace to fall in their entirety into a pattern of imposition and resistance. The mere existence of a charter for the postwar world, agreed upon through a process of multilateral bargaining, not only can bind together victor and vanquished, but can serve as a contract among the victors themselves.

The magnitude of the effort expended to secure victory and the fact that in total war victory comes to be defined in almost purely military terms, however, are prejudicial to securing nonmilitary goals in the postwar period. The resentment of the vanquished toward the victor, nurtured by the sacrifices it has suffered during the war, is exacerbated by the further sacrifices demanded of it. Also proportionate to the totality of victory, the victor is faced with the predicament of finding something of value in the rubble of his opponent's destruction. Furthermore, the victor confronts the dilemma of how to employ his international leverage to secure a transnational transfer of values. As Kenneth Waltz has indicated, "military force, used internationally, is a means of establishing control over a territory, not of exercising control within it."[10] Thus, to the extent that the victor is interested in exercising control within the defeated nation, whether for the purpose of extracting resources, punishing offenders, or establishing the political, social, economic, religious, or ideological conditions dictated by the nature of the total war program, he develops an interest in erecting a leadership with sufficient legitimacy to serve as the fulcrum for the exercise of foreign pressure and influence upon the domestic society. The dilemma of both the victor and such leadership is that its legitimacy is inversely related to its transmission of external coercion.

If this tends to place the new government of the defeated state in a tenuous position, it also creates, under certain circumstances, a unique bargaining situation. On the one hand, facing outward, the government can invoke the extent of domestic resistance to mitigate foreign demands. On the other hand, looking inward, it can invoke fears of more dire consequences to extract elements of compliance. Though it may win the affections of neither constituency, it becomes essential to each.

This, however, is a delicate task. To be all things to all people, to play these contradictory roles without faltering, requires unusual skill and stature. It is hardly surprising that such leadership rarely emerges, for the very nature of the responsibility is such as to drive away those individuals who have the most to lose by being compromised and to attract those opportunists whose very skills of functional schizophrenia have worked to the detriment of their reputations for integrity.

COERCION AND ITS ALTERNATIVES

Ultimately, the ability of the coalition to extract and impose values derives from the vulnerability of the defeated state to the application of additional increments of military force with concomitant pain and destruction. This is the threat, whether explicit or implied, that accompanies every demand. The effectiveness of coercion of this sort depends on two factors: the credibility of the threat and its effective reception. The maintenance of credibility entails both direct and opportunity costs for the victor at a time when pressures for demobilization, reconstruction, and a "return to normalcy" are likely to be at their height, thus further complicating the realization of offensive goals. The effectiveness of a threat and its execution are dependent upon reception by the right party. Fostering disunity in the defeated enemy, disrupting the social fabric so as to fragment the united will to resist can have the undesired consequence of reducing the effectiveness of coercion. If those in a position to respond to coercion are insensitive to the cries of those to whom it is applied, which is more likely when fragmentation occurs, then coercion fails. Since those in control of the most precious values of a society are likely to be those who are least exposed to punishment, their dissociation from the fate of their countrymen can be a liability for the victor, necessitating the costly and morally repulsive escalation of violence to effect minimal levels of effective coercion. Of course, if the opposite is true and a defeated state is highly unified around national or ideological goals, it, too, might be willing to accept very high levels of punishment before acquiescing to what it regards as unconscionable demands. Both alternatives run counter to the victor's desire for maximum acquiescence at minimal cost.

The material and moral costs of effecting compliance are likely to create pressures in the alliance and its units for the use of alternative strategies. This is especially true since the issue shifts for the victors from survival to the extraction and imposition of values, a goal hardly compatible with ever-widening destruction. Furthermore, the relationship of the victorious coalition to the defeated state does not take place in a political vacuum, but in the context of an environment whose national, subnational, or transnational actors might be tempted to engage in predatory actions designed to capitalize on the disruptions effected by the war and its unresolved aftermath. These might take the form of revolutionary activity, security threats to the exhausted victors, or hyena-like encroachments upon the fallen victim.

The common interests of the victors and certain groups among the vanquished in the face of genuine threats or in the exploitation of exaggerated or fabricated fears suggests a means of transcending the victor-vanquished relationship. One alternative for the victors to costly enforcement is to foster voluntary compliance with the essence of the victory program, replacing the stick of national punishment with the carrot of positive incentives to collaborators against a third party. A plausible threat can facilitate the cultivation of a compliant elite willing to serve the victors in the extraction and imposition of values. In return, the victors can assure their agent of special rewards. These might include: support for its domestic authority; concessions to its economic interests; increased autonomy; and reintegration into the international system. Of course, the victors must be careful not to compromise their agent domestically with too great a show of solidarity. Even so, the victor can compensate for the loss of legitimacy which its agent might suffer as it implements its part of the reintegration package by condoning an increase in the agent's authority to repress dissidents. The double hinges for the success of this strategy are: (1) the plausibility of a common threat from a third party sufficient to win the acquiescence of significant segments of the elites and masses in both the victor states and the defeated state and (2) sufficient foresight and flexibility on the part of the leadership of the victor states to abandon unrealistic or peripheral demands and to concentrate upon the essence of the victory program.

These concepts have frequently been invoked in the service of transcending the victor-vanquished relationship. Transnational solidarity among elites has been employed to oppose challenges from below which threaten the existing political and socio-economic order. This was the case with respect to the repression of revolution in Germany following World War I and, less dramatically, with regard to the treatment of political extremists in the states defeated in World War II. The support extended by the individual Allies to moderate German leaders in the post-World War I period and the encouragement of Christian Democracy after World War II also were designed to serve common class interests. Ideological appeals for unity around common values that are perceived to be threatened have been similarly used. Following World War I and World War II, both within Germany and among the Western Allies, the question of Germany's western or eastern alignment was cast partly in terms of ideological values. Perhaps most effective in winning widespread popular support is the discovery or designation of a new security threat upon which victor and vanquished can focus with equal intensity. The Soviet Union served this purpose after both World Wars. Obviously, these sources of reintegration, while logically distinct, frequently overlap in practice.

The successful reintegration of the enemy along lines acceptable to those in control of the victor states and the defeated state is contingent not only on the compatibility of these elites, but on their ability to maintain support for this program among challenging elites and masses. Challenges within the defeated state may be mounted on the charge of treasonous collaboration and abandonment of principle, accompanied with calls for renewed resistance. They may be no more principled than a demand for wider or altered patterns of participation in the spoils of collaboration or a reduction in the burdens of the program of fulfillment. Or they may be based on ideals and values at odds with those that are regarded as responsible for the war and its aftermath. Conversely, challenges within the victor states or among them may be based on accusations of having betrayed the recent dead. Or they may rest on the material dissatisfactions of disfavored groups. On the other hand, dissidents may demand, perhaps even in concert with those sharing their views within the defeated state, "truly" enlightened policies that serve not the interests of the elite, the nation, or the alliance, but their conception of the interests of mankind and future generations. Finally, opposition in both victor and vanquished states can be based upon doubts regarding the credibility or the significance of the integrating principle or upon a combination of self-serving and idealistic elements.

Though treated in a parallel manner, the problem of agreeing upon the nature of the program for reintegration presents distinct problems to the victors and the defeated state. While for the defeated state, or at least its elite, the reintegration project is likely to be preferable to the alternative of punitive coercion, this is not necessarily apparent or true for the victors. Even if it is obvious that reintegration is an optional international arrangement, the leaders in the allied camp must be concerned with the domestic impact of this solution. They must each confront the aroused expectations of their populations, necessarily frustrating certain groups and seeming to favor others. Furthermore, the victors must contend not only with the reduction of overall rewards, but also with the relative distribution of rewards. To some extent, this is determined by the characteristics of the reintegration package, upon which depends the share of tangible and symbolic rewards available to each participant. All those factors that define the separate identity of each of the victors serve to differentiate the relative value or meaning of these benefits. Any solution, necessarily implying compromise and less than complete satisfaction, will tend to open the leadership to the triple accusations of having treated the enemy too leniently, having not received a due share in relation to other allies, and having maldistributed available values among domestic groups.

Whether or not the leaders of the defeated state will agree to the reintegration program will depend upon two calculations. One is the long-term effect upon the nation and the leadership group itself of the marginal melioration in treatment. It is possible that acceptance of short-term pain might appear to be necessary to reduce the long-term costs of the victory program. This is especially true if the leaders of the defeated state perceive the victors' offer as undermining their domestic power or their nation's future efforts to resist demands and to obtain further concessions. Another calculation will be based upon an estimation of the advantages to the state and its governmental elite of other tactics. A show of interest combined with a reluctance to conclude a final agreement might produce incremental improvements in the offer. Obviously the leverage available to the defeated state is, in many respects, a function of the cohesion of the alliance it confronts: the more united the alliance, the weaker the bargaining position of the defeated state. Skillful maneuvering might permit the defeated nation to drive a wedge between jealous and competitive allies. Such an effort might succeed in winning better conditions from the individual allies. More important, however, are the opportunities created inadvertently by allies intent upon transcending the victor-vanquished relationship. Their success in establishing the credibility of a common external threat can have a boomerang effect. For flexible, opportunistic leaders of the defeated state, this might offer a chance to parlay the allies' fear into an important bargaining advantage by threatening to cooperate or ally with the outcast third force. Or, in actually doing so, the leadership of the defeated state might find a new basis for resistance.

THE STABILITY AND COSTS OF PEACE

To the utility of total conventional war for defensive purposes corresponds the relative futility of such actions for offensive purposes. There is no question that total conventional war might be a necessary response to foreign aggressions which threaten the nation or its core values. Expectations of securing offensive goals through an Armageddon, including expectations that arise in the course of an essentially defensive struggle, are likely to meet with a variety of frustrations. Such goals contain their own contradictions.

A Carthaginian peace can only be maintained at great cost to both the victor and the vanquished. In the victor state, these costs are likely to breed dissatisfaction and factiousness that weaken its security posture. In the vanquished state, these costs are likely to breed a spirit of resistance and revenge that will further strain the resources and resolve of the victor. The costs to the vanquished state itself are implicit in, and defined by, the nature of a retributive peace.

The least stable and most costly peace is likely to evolve from a situation where security measures are haphazardly or unevenly applied and significant segments of the defeated state's population are antagonized by the foreign imposition of an exploitative exchange of values. Such a situation can evolve incrementally from the time overt hostilities are concluded. Victors might falsely assume that not only their defensive goals, but their offensive ones as well, will be self-executing. Disabused of this illusion by the resistance of the vanquished, they will be tempted to engage in acts of coercion. The costliness of such action and the difficulty involved in communicating threats effectively may lead them to transcend the victor-vanquished relationship by providing benefits to cooperative elites in the vanquished state in return for fulfillment of the essence of the victory program. There are risks involved, however, in emphasizing the common threat posed by a third party in order to facilitate and lend credibility to such a reintegration package. Such a solution can strengthen the ability of the former antagonist to resist measures vital to the victor's security. For example, the new danger can serve as a weighty argument on the part of the defeated state in favor of rearmament for foreign or domestic police actions or in favor of a more active foreign policy, and it can open the prospect of a diplomatic realignment of the outcasts. At the same time, such a deal can provide benefits that alienate the domestic forces in both the victor and the vanquished states at whose expense it is concluded.

In the victor state, nationalists and class-conscious masses will probably resent the sacrifice of defensive goals for the attainment of offensive ones. In the defeated state, it is unlikely that those who bear the greatest burden of the obligation to fulfill the modified victory program will be favorably impressed by the political and economic advantages they thereby purchase for a narrow elite.

A more generous peace, of course, is one in which offensive goals are less prominent in the victory program. Though such a peace may work to the long-run advantage of the victor, there is no guarantee that the sacrifice or the relative absence of offensive goals will necessarily improve its future security situation. The determinants of competition and hostility might be so deeply rooted in geopolitical juxtaposition, historical, cultural, social, economic, or ideological rivalry as to make it impossible to achieve a peaceful coexistence, especially in the wake of a conclusive victory.

The problem is a thorny one for the victor, but one which perhaps is not well served by the dichotomy of a Carthaginian and a generous peace. For a generous peace need not be a lax peace. In this regard, the success of American policies toward Japan following World War II provides an instructive contrast to Allied treatment of Germany after World War I. The most stable and least costly peace is that which combines severity in the enforcement of defensive goals vital to the security of the victor with tolerance and respect for the diversity of other values of the vanquished.

Under these conditions, reintegration of the defeated state can proceed as a function of convergent values. Meanwhile, the rational application of security conditions can serve to protect the victor against a resurgence of the enemy at a justifiable and predictable cost. At the same time, the defeated state will have an explicit and credible guideline as to the limits of tolerable divergence from the established international regime. In that such an arrangement does not partake of a transnational alliance of elites against elements of their own populations, it is likely to win the support of those sectors of the population in both the victor and vanquished states that place defensive goals above partisan advantage.

THE FRUITS OF VICTORY IN WORLD WAR I

The following case study is intended to illustrate the previous analysis. In contrast to the general framework presented above, it focuses narrowly upon the victor-vanquished relationship after World War I. Its scope

extends from 1919 to 1925, from the Versailles Conference to the Locarno Conference, and refers to the entirety of Allied-German inter-
actions. But it is concerned more specifically with Franco-German relations in 1921–1922, a period that began with Lenin's inauguration of the
New Economic Policy (NEP) and the First London Conference on reparations and that ended with the Cannes and Genoa Conferences and the
German-Soviet Treaty at Rapallo. Its emphasis is upon the dilemmas confronted by French governments, assuming the multiple roles of victor, ally,
national actor, and national leader, in deriving tangible benefits from
military victory.

The wartime alliance against Germany was based upon common strategic opposition to the expansive aims of the enemy. Though Britain,
France, the United States, Italy, and the other Allies shared certain ideological, economic, social, and cultural values, theirs was essentially a
minimal defensive coalition. Russia's participation contradicted the
broader purposes which were articulated as the war progressed and expanded. These aims were designed to justify the unexpected degree of
carnage and to imbue the emerging Pyrrhic victory with meaning.

The alliance did not survive the war intact, and it was further dismembered following the peace. The rupture of international bonds was
partially a consequence of the strains of war upon domestic unity. In
Britain, France, and the United States, dissension was contained by a
combination of repression and appeals to patriotism. In Italy, the tensions
of the war and the bankruptcy of victory tore apart the fragile and un-
integrated polity. Fragmentation was most serious in Russia, weakening
the hold of the *ancien regime* and opening the way to a successful revolution in the very course of the war. The Russian Revolution, and the peace
concluded between the Bolsheviks and the Germans, presented Russia's
former allies with strategic problems and with a situation they regarded
as threatening to their political, socio-economic, and ideological values.
By the time of the Versailles Conference, the Russian question was nearly
as central as the German one to the statesmen who met to establish
Europe's postwar regime.

A basic divergence among the Allies with regard to their postwar aims
was manifested as early as the Versailles Conference. Although in the
flush of victory they managed to veil their divisions, these became more
obtrusive in the years that followed. The nature of the total war Europe
had experienced led statesmen to the conclusion that economic and
ideological mobilization were essential components of overall strategy.

This stimulated the development by each state of a comprehensive security program which was rooted in the distinctive nexus of interests and values defining the "national situation."[11] Naturally, the integral conception of these programs created significant barriers to compromise and accommodation.

France's view of its security requirements led to demands for a harshly retributive and militarized peace. Britain and the United States were inclined to be more lenient. They favored the restoration of the European balance of power by the gradual reintegration of Germany. They were motivated by the determination to prevent a power vacuum in Central Europe and by a desire to reestablish prewar commercial and financial patterns, in which Germany had played an important role. They were reluctant to see France exercise Continental hegemony. Furthermore, they were troubled by the examples of the Russian, German, and Hungarian revolutions, for they feared the spread of bolshevism. The peace that emerged from this division was a patchwork quilt of compromises and contradictions. Germany, which signed the treaty only under the duress of military defeat, was partially dismembered, partially occupied, and largely demilitarized. It was placed under an obligation to pay large, but unspecified, sums of reparations. On the other hand, the formal mechanism for enforcing the conditions of the peace and the procedures by which Allied disagreements were to be settled was left quite vague. To complicate matters further, the United States Senate's repudiation of the efforts of President Wilson signaled a reversion by the most powerful ally to its traditional posture of eschewing foreign political involvements.

This left Britain and France responsible for the enforcement of the Versailles Treaty. Many interests divided these two allies. Strategically, Britain was an insular power, less exposed than France to a German military resurgence. Economically, Britain was far more dependent than France upon trade with Germany and a reconstructed Continent. The enormous destruction which France suffered as a result of having fought the war on its own soil led it to count upon German reparations for general economic recovery and for the reconstruction of the devastated areas in the north and the east. These very reparations, the British feared, would debilitate Germany to the detriment of their "devastated area": the commercial sector of their economy. To the French, who suffered from a sense of demographic and economic inferiority to their eastern neighbor, the reduction of Germany's material potential to wage modern war was of strategic as well as economic significance. Ideologically, the leaders of both France and Britain were opposed to revolutionary social change. But while Britain found its ideological opposition to Russia reinforced by a history of strategic antagonism, particularly in South Asia and the Straits, the cornerstone of French security policy had been based upon the Russian alliance. Even in the postwar period, the French often asserted that no fundamental conflicts of national interest stood between them and their erstwhile ally. With respect to Germany, Britain's fear of the consequences of revolutionary activity led it to urge moderation in the enforcement of certain demilitarization provisions. France, however, was far too alarmed at the possibility of the military recovery of a Germany of any political complexion to accept Britain's advice. Domestically, the political elites of both Britain and France were divided on several major issues. The British elite was far more troubled than the French over the possibility of serious class conflict, and it was, therefore, more inclined to accommodate internationally to reduce domestic tensions. The divisions in France, however, were sharpened rather than softened by the prospect of international accommodation. The Versailles Treaty constituted a formula for foreign policy consensus among Frenchmen, and any obvious departure from this postwar charter was viewed as a sacrifice of national rights.

These contradictory perspectives were moderated in some respects by mutual dependence, but the difficulties of translating them into policy were exacerbated by this same relationship. The leaders of Britain and France realized that their countries formed a natural security community. Even this shared perception, however, was partial, applying only to the contingency of westward German aggression. From the British Isles, peace appeared divisible. Britain did not consider Eastern Europe to be worth fighting for, and at times it almost seemed to invite Germany to redirect its aggressive energies to the East. The French, on the other hand, were wedded to a Continental policy of encirclement which was given form by the replacement of the Russian alliance with a series of treaty obligations to the successor regimes.

The French found that to win British support in any one area of policy they were expected to make concessions in others that proved difficult or impossible in the rekindled atmosphere of domestic factionalism. To act in an independent or autarkic manner required a costly mobilization of will and resources which the dispirited and ravaged nation could ill afford. Furthermore, failure in such an enterprise inevitably would increase future dependence upon coordinated policies with Britain. The British, meanwhile, were also in a difficult situation. The French demanded meaningful concessions of them which they were reluctant to grant. Failure to satisfy them, however, meant that the French would act alone in a manner which, regardless of its success or failure, would stymie British policy.

Germany, which had been the catalytic agent in European politics since the age of Bismarck, found itself reduced to a rather helpless condition after the war, an object of the actions of others. Though its masses may have been deceived by military propaganda, its leaders comprehended the magnitude of Germany's defeat. They understood the extent of the state's isolation and of its vulnerability to the armies of its enemies. The nation whose fortunes had risen, and fallen, on a policy of *Grossmacht*, fueled with blood and iron, was now forced to learn a humbler politics: the politics of weakness. For strategy, its leaders were forced to substitute delicate tactical maneuvers to meet contingencies shaped abroad. Instead of rattling sabres, they had to appeal to humanitarian sympathies and look for conflicts between British and French interests which might be exploited to German advantage. The language of assertion had to be replaced with that of compliance and goodwill. The cult of power and action had to give way to a seeming docility and passivity, combined with cunning and ruse. Pride and honor had to yield to the virtues of survival.

These were difficult lessons to learn. Yet Germany adapted well, or well enough, in the years of 1919–1925. The process was marked by catastrophic vicissitudes, but there is no doubt that by the time of the Locarno Conference Germany was in a far stronger diplomatic position than it was at any time since the war, that it had managed to moderate or evade the harshest terms of the peace, and, in the process, to rob from the allies the inflated benefits they had anticipated as a reward for victory. The flight of the German phoenix is an illustration of the futilities of an attempt to translate even a conclusive decision on the battlefield into meaningful, long-term advantage.

Germany was powerless to resist Britain and France physically. Its recovery of diplomatic standing and economic health was due to bargaining advantages other than its historically vaunted military capabilities. These were the endowments of nature, the skills and industry of the population, and the particular opportunities of the postwar environment.

Although crushed militarily, Germany's economic infrastructure emerged almost intact from the war. As the champion of European recovery, Britain recognized an important shared interest with Germany in revitalizing German industry and European trade. Even France, which preferred to focus on French reconstruction (for which it depended upon German reparations) was forced grudgingly to acknowledge the interest of a creditor in the well-being of its debtor. This dependence was reinforced by a need for Ruhr coke with which to stoke the iron furnaces of Lorraine. Widespread protectionist sentiment in French industry, and economic nationalism in government, encouraged the conclusion of agreements with Germany for the restriction of competition through the allocation of markets and the limitation of production. The conflicting economic policies of Britain and France as well as conflict between industrial, commercial, and financial elites within these two states gave Germany a lever with which to pry for concessions.

So, too, did the fear of revolution and the combination of ideological and strategic antagonism toward Soviet Russia with a widespread interest in its economic exploitation. Britain was acutely sensitive to the possibility that strict adherence to the Versailles peace might stimulate dangerous and infectious revolutionary activity within Germany. Thereforce, it attempted to exert a moderating influence on France's policy of enforcement. Germany's leaders exploited this fear, and they also attempted to profit from Germany's crucial position between East and West in the larger context of the "international civil war."[12] Bismarck's policy served as a guideline, for he had realized that the dangers of encirclement by a hostile alliance were counterbalanced by diplomatic advantages for Germany in times of tension between Russia and the West. Allied policies toward Russia in the wake of the Russian Revolution certainly played into German hands.

Finally, an additional trump was the consequence of the different strategic interests identified by an insular Britain and a Continental France. The friction produced by several failures to revive their alliance with a guarantee treaty contributed to a divisiveness which was useful to Germany. It ended only when Germany was brought into the settlement during the Locarno Conference, at the cost of important concessions by the Allies.

One of the most remarkable features of the international system in the postwar period was its fluidity. The ten years that preceded the war had been marked by increasing polarization between the two groups of states that eventually clashed. At Paris, the peace conference drew a sharp distinction between victor and vanquished and gave to the former the benefits of the burdens placed on the latter. Almost immediately, however, issues arose which cut across this neat configuration; the wisdom and the possibility of its maintenance soon were questioned. For if there were vested interests in the defense of the Versailles order, there were also interests in its modification or abrogation. To many individuals and nations, it seemed that a retributive peace was the surest guarantee of a future war of revenge. Furthermore, such a settlement accorded poorly with a solution to Europe's pressing economic problems.

The pattern of international politics in Europe between Versailles and Locarno was shaped by a fundamental contradiction which had contributed to the outbreak of the war and which was exacerbated by the circumstances of its settlement. The expansive drive of Europe's advanced economies was aimed at the creation of a world market and an international division of labor. But private economic power also sought to secure control over the institutions of the state so as to establish a legal and political regime propitious to its interests. Thus the integrating tendencies of economic forces clashed with the firm divisions of national boundaries. The resulting competitive protectionism and economic nationalism played an important role in heightening international tensions in the prewar period, both within Europe and in colonial rivalry. After the war, Europe was even more divided politically. Three empires dissolved and, in their places, a host of independent new states was created. The Versailles system aggravated the rupture between the Allies and Germany as well as between the West and Soviet Russia. Furthermore, it was both a manifestation and a source of dissension among the allies themselves. Not only did the war contribute to political fragmentation, but it also was responsible for the inflammation of nationalist sentiments. Postwar chauvinism combined with ideological conflicts to reinforce the significance of geographic divisions. Europe's common legacy in the postwar period was physical destruction and economic dislocation. Enlightened statesmen and businessmen realized that reconstruction and economic revival required innovative, cooperative ventures which ignored national borders. The need for economic reintegration was never greater, yet the crosspurposes of national policies were rarely more marked.

The clash of political and economic imperatives was the pivot of European politics in the years 1919–1925. It was expressed in the form of three derivative contradictions. The requirements of Europe's economies conflicted with divergent national security policies and with both nationalist and class-based ideologies, just as security goals and ideologies themselves were poorly aligned. The configurations of European diplomacy between Versailles and Locarno were products of attempts to arrange these elements. The significance of Locarno is that it served as a temporary synthesis, a point of balance in a moving disequilibrium.

SECURITY

As with most nations at most times, security was the most important of France's long-range goals. Its relative position in the hierarchy of French postwar values is less clear. In part, this derives from semantic obscurity. One of the lessons of World War I was that in a long war economic and demographic strength are convertible into firepower and manpower. Afterward, many strategists expanded their traditional security concerns to include not merely borders, armies, and equipment, but the fundamental health of the economy, and particularly of heavy industry. At the same time, the transnational challenge to the legitimacy of governments added an ideological element to security questions. In this broader sense, all the major issues merge, and the concept of security becomes interchangeable with a definition of national purpose. To avoid the tautologies such usage might foster, it is desirable to restrict the term to its most usual employment in the postwar period; that is, as a euphemism for military security against German attack. What was the extent of French preoccupation with this narrower meaning of security? William Jordan has stated that "from the first months of peace the French viewed the renewal of war as a very real danger of the immediate future."[13] Arnold Wolfers has claimed, though, that the "French were not concerned about the near future . . ."[14] Indeed, arguments can be produced in support of each assertion. Certainly, the French were demoralized by the war, they were fearful of German revenge, and they knew that Germany was larger and potentially richer than France. The French accumulated as many political safeguards as possible at Versailles. Afterward, their alliance system in Eastern Europe and their attempt to secure a British guarantee indicated an obsession with security. On the other hand, the occupation of the Rhineland, control of the Saar, and Germany's disarmament, geographical dismemberment, political disorder, and economic disintegration made fears for the immediate future totally irrational, if not paranoid, on the part of the strongest power on the Continent. This is true during the early postwar years even when, taking account of France's support for the whole structure of the status quo based on Versailles, including the Cental European settlement, French anxiety is understood as "that of a nation with responsibilities and ambitions truly continental in character and extent."[15] There is no evidence in the archives of the Quai d'Orsay[16] which would indicate that the security fixation was anything but future-oriented. It was unthinkable that Germany could reopen hostilities or in any way challenge French military dominance in the "immediate future." Yet it is true that the dangers of a not-too-remote time, pictured in French nightmares as shortly following the fifteen-year occupation of the Rhineland, struck fear into the French and influenced their foreign policy outlook throughout the interim.

Both Wolfers and Jordan have characterized the difference in French and British conceptions of security by stressing that the emphasis in Britain lay on the prevention of war, and hence the British advocated the conciliation of Germany and its reintegration into the European system.[17] France, on the other hand, was pictured as fatalistic and anxious to prepare in advance for a common defense which would take effect at the very outset of war, so as to prevent hostilities on French soil. However valid the insight, the contrast these two authors have drawn is too stark, particularly for the early postwar years and under the foreign policy leadership of the French Center-Left. In fact, with regard to the restricted meaning of security, there was really no divergence between the Center-Left and the Right. Raymond Poincaré tried as assiduously as did Aristide Briand to obtain a meaningful guarantee treaty from Britain, and he wholeheartedly supported Briand's policy in Eastern Europe. The different climate of France's relations with Britain and Germany under Briand and Poincaré stemmed from their contrasting views of security, broadly conceived. The same problems of enforcing the Versailles Treaty as insurance against a hostile German resurgence confronted both the Center-Left and the Right. In principle, both domestic groups were as willing to explore means for the prevention of war through conciliation as Britain, provided that these did not entail an abandonment of more concrete guarantees. This proviso, however, was subjected to different interpretations. Realizing the extent of German recalcitrance, Briand sought to interest Germany in fulfillment by providing incentives, whether in the form of economic entente or European reconstruction, were specially chosen from expansion sectors so as not to reduce France's rights under the treaty or allow Germany to gain an advantage relative to France. They were seen as the least painful means for Germany to comply with the reparations provisions of Versailles. By linking the French and German economic sectors, they promised to give France additional leverage with the German government, to provide rewards to important sectors of French industry, and to create a common interest in functional cooperation. In comparison with the substantial achievement of the spirit of the Versailles Treaty which the Briand government hoped to attain with this program, the concessions that would have to be made on its most unenforceable sections were regarded as minor. This was especially so if, as the Briand government hoped and calculated, these policies won from Britain a guarantee of French security. Poincaré was more legalistic about the treaty and more skeptical about the advantages of compromise. Germany had lost the war, and France's future security depended upon the enforcement of a punitive peace that stripped its past—and possibly its future—enemy of the means to wage modern warfare. Whereas Briand directed his efforts against the psychological sources of German militarism, Poincaré took aim at its industrial and economic bases. Even if this attitude alienated Britain, Poincaré had no doubt that common interests would suffice to guarantee France at least as much support as Britain was willing to offer in a formal treaty. Of course, he would have compromised if Britain had been willing to negotiate a new alliance, but anything less was regarded as inconsequential.

In spite of this display of a considerable degree of independence, the ineluctable reality of France's ultimate dependence on Britain confronted governments of all persuasions with an inflexible limitation on diplomacy. France's geographical proximity to Germany and Britain's insularity were reflected in their respective psychological distance from perceived security threats. The French, naturally, were more sensitive to developments with possible adverse consequences, and they acted as sentinels, often sounding warnings and expressing alarm on the theory that an excess of vigilance was preferable to the slightest neglect. The British frequently turned their hostility against the bearer of bad tidings, since the only reports they wished to hear were those that confirmed their predispositions in favor of a harmonious restoration of normal relationships. Thus, despite the common Franco-British interest in the prevention of security threats from Germany in the West, the French realized that they were consigned to play the role of supplicants before the British arbiters. And whether they accepted their lot with grace or resentment did not alter the unequal relationship.

France felt even more vulnerable because of its interests in, and commitments to, the new states of Eastern Europe. Although at Versailles

Britain had helped to construct the *cordon sanitaire* for the containment of Communist and German expansion, in the postwar world it refused to accept responsibilities for the maintenance of the Central European status quo against Germany. Unlike France, Britain did not preoccupy itself with the fate of the states caught between the revisionist powers. It was especially scornful of the viability and internal structure of Poland. Its major goal in the area, revealed at the time of the Battle of Warsaw, actually was to protect Germany and hence Europe against the spread of bolshevism. Its stand in favor of Germany, and against France and Poland, on the dispute over Upper Silesia was cast mainly in terms of reparations. But it was indicative of a general attitude that served as precedent and foundation for the appeasement doctrine, introduced much later. From Britain's point of view, the Continental balance of power was in disequilibrium due to French dominance and the inferiority imposed on Germany by the Versailles Treaty. A power vacuum in Eastern Europe invited incursions by Soviet Russia once it had recovered from the effects of its revolution, the foreign interventions, the civil war, and the famine. An orderly restoration of German influence, therefore, was desirable. Britain's economic interests and ideological purposes complemented this goal. However, once recovered, Germany might pose a threat in the West unless other outlets were found for its political and economic energies. Britain thus carefully discriminated between its theoretical willingness to underwrite security in the West and its categorical refusal to encircle Germany simultaneously from the East. Of course, this policy was antithetical to that of France, which sought in Eastern Europe a bastion to replace the Russian alliance. Whereas Britain had come to see the European peace as divisible, France feared that Germany's aggrandizement in the East merely would strengthen it for war against France. Thus France clung to the barbed wire concept of Eastern Europe, while Britain seemed to transmute the analogy to that of a single-edged blade directed toward the East.

France, of course, was no more immune than Britain from the influence of ideology on its security perspective. After all, this is the obvious explanation for the abandonment of the Russian alliance in favor of strategic interdependence with Eastern Europe. Arnold Wolfers argued otherwise: "in the early post-war years an alliance with the Soviet Union was neither necessary nor desirable from the French point of view."[18] In fact, he claimed, "the only French objective with regard to Soviet Russia was to isolate and remove her as far as possible from the regions in which France had established her preponderance." Wolfers rejected the contention that French policy was the product of a class-conscious bourgeoisie which resented its financial losses and feared the spread of communism. He pointed to the reversal of the French position in 1934, despite Stalin's policies and the absence of a debt settlement. In light of the contributions of the Russian alliance to French security from the time of its signing until the Revolution, Wolfers ought to have offered some proof for the assertion that, in the postwar period, a similar bond would not have been desirable for reasons independent of ideological considerations. Wolfers argued that Russia's weakness and Germany's prostration and encircle-ment in the early 1920's reduced the desirability and necessity of an alliance. However, if, as Wolfers also argued, France did not anticipate war in the near future, then obviously Russia's war potential after recovery exceeded that of the Eastern European states. The fact is that Germany's weakness made any Eastern alliance something of an insurance policy against the future and not an objective necessity in the early postwar years. Thus, Wolfers's line of reasoning is circular: France did not need Russia because it could count on Eastern Europe. Why France chose to put its premiums into Eastern Europe, why it found alliances with those states more desirable than with Russia is left unexplained once ideological arguments are rejected. Wolfers's basis for rejecting them was flimsy also. On the one hand, he ignored the ideological climate in France in the postwar period, as well as the economic grievances of the propertied classes (which resulted from the Soviet ideology) justifying confiscation. On the other hand, he made no place in his argument for the heightened sense of danger from Germany, shared by France and Russia, which paved the way for a temporary ideological truce after Hitler rose to power.

ECONOMICS

If security was the most important of France's long-range aims, ques-tions of economics were the most complex and pressing of immediate concerns. Their complexity, on the international level, was the conse-quence of the different quality of economic adversity which the war inflicted on each of the major powers and the conflict of foreign economic policies with which they attempted to correct these situations. France suffered enormous physical and human destruction, which it sought to remedy by obtaining reparations. Britain suffered a severe economic crisis and high unemployment as a result of the collapse of European trade, the restoration of which became its top priority. The turmoil in Russia resulted in economic ruin, which the Bolsheviks tried to overcome with a bizarre combination of socialism, capitalism (NEP), and an appeal to foreign investors and traders. Ironically, Germany's economic structure and infrastructure were affected less than those of the victors. The Versailles Treaty, however, attempted to correct this situation by taking away territory and economic resources and by placing Germany under an obligation to pay an indefinite, but huge, sum in reparations. Caught between Allied demands and the systematic recalcitrance of powerful industrialists at home, the weak German government alternately appealed for mercy and expressed scorn or defiance, offered and withheld fulfillment of the treaty, and generally tried to survive, by cunning and evasion, a situation it was powerless to master.

Resolution of the obvious contradictions in national outlooks was further complicated because international economic questions had direct and easily perceived material consequences for influential segments of domestic society. Consequently, the measure of discord or cooperation which characterized international economic relations was a function of the compatibility of the economic interests represented by the different governments. One factor which mitigated conflict, however, and which accounts for the continual search for broad solutions, was that the welfare of each individual state was inseparable from some resolution of an international situation which all deplored. Nevertheless, the various plans for general accommodation failed, one after the other, due to the impossibility of reconciling interests that diverged so widely. The result was a series of partial and inadequate expedients which satisfied no state and only worsened their common plight.

From one perspective, France's share of responsibility for this state of affairs was considerable. Its autarkic tendencies conflicted with its insistence upon maximizing reparations. This contradiction was a major source of European economic conflict. A different view, however, would emphasize the justice of French claims, Germany's subversion of its treaty obligations, and the encouragement it derived from Britain. Britain's righteous denunciation of France for bringing calamity to the European economic system would be balanced with a recollection of Britain's role in undermining the cooperative tendencies in Franco-German economic relations. Neither view is without merit, which is an indication that the fault was systemic in nature, the product of national crosspurposes. The luxury to adopt such a disengaged outlook, however, was denied to policy-makers, who were forced to deal in rationalizations and justifications of their own policies and condemnation or disparagement of conflicting schemes of rival states.

To a major power, the international system does not present itself as an abstract and unchangeable situation but rather as a field for action and as a product of previous acts. While the small power faces a situation analogous to that of an individual buyer or seller in an economic model of pure competition, where the conditions of the market must be accepted as givens, the major power has some of the characteristics of the oligopolist who must accept certain limitations, largely those imposed by the other members of his exclusive club, but who can help shape other important features of the environment in which he operates. Unlike the more constant arrangement of security and ideological factors which France confronted in the international environment, economic issues were distinctly more mutable. In the year 1921–1922, France alternated between two very different economic policies. The Briand government, before the Second London Conference, and the Poincaré government, in the early months of 1922, each assumed a hard-line position. Between the Second London Conference and his resignation after the Cannes Conference, however, Briand's policy was far more flexible and conciliatory. The Second London Conference was a moment of truth for the Center-Left, which was forced to choose between employing its freedom to deal independently with Germany and maintaining the appearance, at least, of Allied unity and the goodwill of Britain. Briand skillfully saved face with a veiled and graceful capitulation. The lesson he learned from the experience was that France would do well to avoid reliance upon Britain in its economic relations with Germany and, instead, proceed to regulate problems directly with its adversary by fostering common interests. The Wiesbaden Agreement, providing for the delivery of reparations in kind, and diverse plans for industrial ententes or stock distributions were the outgrowth of this changed attitude. Domestic resistance, German delays, and Britain's hostility to economic alliances from which it was excluded undermined these efforts. But Britain's proposed alternative, European reconstruction, which aimed at the exploitation of the Russian market, shared many of the same premises. While it omitted the marriage of coal and iron and the rationalization of production, the division of markets, and the moderation of competition, it was based upon the international cooperation of industry, and was directed toward an expansion sector in order to provide Germany with a means of paying reparations without inundating Western markets.[19] The diagnosis of the capitalists was that Europe needed new and undeveloped outlets for trade and investment.

Fundamentally different economic interests divided France and Britain on the issues of the postwar period, both on the level of broad programs and in specifics. Of course, there existed a solid base of trade that worked to mutual advantage, but this had come to be taken largely for granted. On unresolved subjects, the two nations were usually in contention. France was determined to receive the maximum possible amount of reparations. The British were anxious to restore Germany as a commercial partner. They regarded French demands as excessive and likely to lead the German economy to a catastrophe, with dire results for Britain. They were apprehensive of cooperative policies, as well. They resented the progressive loss of their Continental coal market, and, while the French iron industry demanded more coke for its underutilized furnaces, the British attempted to make German coal more expensive in order to increase the competitiveness of their own product. They feared the combined power of Franco-German heavy industry and were determined to frustrate plans for mergers and cartels that would have placed their industries at a disadvantage on world markets. The proposal for European reconstruction was designed to avoid the major pitfalls of previous solutions. Through this plan for tripartite cooperation in Russia, Britain hoped to restore Germany in a controlled manner, provide France with reparations, and assure profitable outlets for excess production and capital, without losing economic influence on the Continent. Briand was about to agree to this ingenious scheme at the Cannes Conference when he was toppled from power by the Right, which was more ideologically inflexible and more representative of those with economic claims against Russia. Finally, Russia's refusal to serve as the unequal partner in a plan that it correctly perceived as an attempt to infiltrate the economic sector as a first step in weakening the political bases of its new society condemned to failure the British proposal for general appeasement. Europe had come full circle in its attempt to resolve its economic contradictions.

France's economic relations with Germany followed a sequence similar to the Franco-British relationship. The period between the Second London Conference and the Cannes Conference, in which common purposes flourished, contrasted sharply with the broader framework of conflict. The perennial attributes of Franco-German diplomacy require less explanation than this aberration. Historically, the national aims of each country had been defined largely in opposition to the other. Their pact of hatred, fear, and envy was signed in blood when they again went to war in 1914. At Versailles, the victors sought to restore the vitality of their cadaverous economies with massive transfusions of wealth forcibly extracted from Germany. In the postwar years, Germany blanched at the very prospect of being drained to the extent envisaged by the French reparations program and put up the type of resistance characteristic of the weak but determined. Procrastination and evasion were carried out under the cloak of good faith and fulfillment, amid protestations of inability, rather than unwillingness, to pay. British and American revisionist biases provided Germany with a ploy. It could play off the Allies, one against the other, to prevent their united pressure. But as long as Britain showed respect for the treaty, the French were scrupulous to avoid open divisions that would encourage the Germans. Lloyd George's faint-heartedness at the Second London Conference, however, demonstrated to Briand the limits of Britain's commitment to the reparations provisions. Once the British stance was clarified under crisis conditions, three roads were open to the French: (1) they could defy the British and enforce the treaty independently, (2) they could continue to make accommodations to the British viewpoint and modify their demands, or (3) they could by-pass Britain in order to achieve a direct rapprochement with Germany. The first was the path chosen by Poincaré, the last was the way Briand decided to meet the problem. His failure, partly due to the British, eventually forced him to abandon his course and fall back on the second alternative. But, grasping for a solution, he lost his hold upon the domestic political system, which had come to demand what Poincaré offered.

The Franco-German economic rapprochement reached a peak in the summer and fall of 1921. Three distinct plans received serious consideration: industrial alliances based upon negotiated agreements; complicated shareholding plans that would have settled reparations accounts by a distribution of equity, profits, and control in German firms to French companies through their governments; and delivery of reparations payments in kind. Only the third plan was translated into reality. In form, it was merely a convenient way to avoid the specie transfer problems posed by the reparations clauses of the Versailles Treaty. In spirit, however, it represented considerably more. To Louis Loucheur and Walter Rathenau, who signed the agreement, it signified the first step in the establishment of cooperative economic links between the two countries. It was based on the functionalist premise that gradual integration of the two economies and interpenetration of interests and values would contribute to future peace. Later in the decade, Briand and Loucheur went even further: the former calling for a United States of Europe and the latter proposing far broader plans for economic integration. The ideas behind the diplomatic initiative of 1921 represented the essence of these future schemes. At the very center of these proposals, from the time of Wiesbaden to the present Common Market, lay the marriage of coal and iron. Remarriage, perhaps, would be a more appropriate term, for the foundation of Franco-German unity depended upon the restoration of the natural and mutually beneficial ties between the iron industries of Lorraine and the coal suppliers of the Ruhr that had been developed during the period of German hegemony between 1871 and 1918. All of the negotiations for economic entente began from this assumption and expanded from this basis to include alliances of other heavy industries, most notably chemical and dye manufacturers, and then, almost as an afterthought, the other business and agricultural constituencies whose support was necessary for political success.

Unfortunately for them, the enlightened conservatives who attempted to resolve the antagonism between their two countries underestimated the resistance their plans would encounter, even on the part of some of those who were intended as the prime beneficiaries. Militant hostility toward Germany, narrowly conceived economic interests, and the illusion that the benefits of integration could be achieved without concessions, through a forceful policy of dominance, contributed to the mixed French reception of Wiesbaden and condemned it to failure. As long as the alternative of occupying the Ruhr militarily remained unexplored, many industrialists who would have achieved partial satisfaction through Wiesbaden joined with bellicose elements in opposition to a compromise of any sort. Briand and Loucheur were ahead of their times and their legislative majority. They could not carry out a policy that Britain opposed without solid support at home. And, to complete the vicious circle, British opposition to Wiesbaden gave encouragement to German industrialists to continue their resistance and to hold out for even better terms of settlement. Their attitude was taken in France as further evidence of deceptiveness and was used as an argument against Wiesbaden.

Briand was about to accept Britain's package deal at the Cannes Conference, including the provisions for European reconstruction, when he was recalled to Paris. Although Wiesbaden never was abandoned formally, a major reason for Britain's attraction to the European reconstruction idea was that it superseded the more exclusive Franco-German entente. How significant was this concession from Briand's view-point? The fact that Wiesbaden never had generated great enthusiasm indicates that compromise with Britain, quite likely, was expedient—especially so when it is noted that in August 1921 a French plan had been developed for a Franco-German entente which specifically had anticipated expansionist endeavors in Russia with which Britain would be associated. The European reconstruction plan, it is true, reversed the order in which these goals would be pursued, thus giving Britain a greater role in Franco-German affairs. There was no fundamental contradiction, though, between the two programs. Each sought to harmonize the economies of the states of the West by opening the East to expansion.

When Poincaré came to power, following Briand's resignation, it was with a mandate to reverse the conciliatory trend in French foreign policy and to reassert France's rights under the treaty. In other words, Poincaré endorsed Briand's original program, from before the Second London Conference. But, whereas Briand temporized between his loyalty to the treaty and the maintenance of Allied unity, Poincaré's priorities were clearer. It is not that he did not wish to maintain the ties with Britain. He did, but not at the price of the substantive interests that he believed these ties ought to support. Poincaré's intransigent position reduced Franco-German relations to the nadir of 1921, after the punitive occupation of the Ruhr cities of Duisburg, Ruhrort, and Düsseldorf and during the hostilities in Upper Silesia. To the French Right, Poincaré was successful in rupturing illusions; to the French Left he seemed to perpetuate the illusion that France could act in isolation to enforce the reparations settlement on Germany. Certainly he undermined the position of those who stood in favor of fulfillment in Germany. It could be argued that he merely unmasked their hypocritical attempts to avoid payment in full through a policy of collaboration. But this would miss the reality that in so doing he helped to discredit the only leaders who offered even partial payment and stiffened the already widespread opposition to the treaty. Legally he was right, but politically he reinforced the antipathies and the sense of national unity in resistance that would cost France so dearly in its Ruhr misadventure.

The broad and deep economic and financial ties which underlay the prewar Franco-Russian alliance were sundered by the consequences of the revolution. In the postwar years, there were no economic relations between the two states, and questions of economics were entwined hopelessly with political issues.[20] Whereas the different exigencies of their respective situations led Britain and Germany to adopt practical attitudes toward economic relations with the Soviets, France's position on these issues was nearly as pure and principled as its political and ideological hostility. In some ways this was paradoxical. Frenchmen had lost enormous sums of money through expropriations and unredeemed bonds. For political reasons, their government would seem to have had the greatest stake in obtaining partial repayment through a general settlement.

Several factors account for French behavior. Unlike Britain, France found lucrative outlets for its investment capital in its own devastated areas and in Eastern Europe, and its economic well-being was less dependent upon foreign trade. Unlike Germany, it felt no compelling diplomatic pressure to bury its differences with the Soviets, and in fact its policy in Eastern Europe dictated several good reasons for not doing so. Furthermore, any government that encouraged the numerous French creditors of Russia to accept partial reimbursement would have had to be prepared to face their disillusionment at their partial losses. Anti-Soviet and anti-Communist policies and ideologies had been too oversold to permit a speedy reversal without expectations of substantial advantages. More than any other issue, Briand's readiness to compromise on the Russian question was the cause for his upset. From this, Poincaré learned where the political center of gravity lay, and he refused to endanger his ministry by venturing beyond the point of safety. The fact that he clung to this position at the time of the Genoa Conference, despite the fact that it imperiled the conference and French relations with Britain and that it seemed to create propitious circumstances for a Russo-German entente, demonstrated the extent of his commitment as well as the pitiable illusions and impotent perverseness of French foreign policy.

IDEOLOGY

Ideological conflict in the postwar world had important diplomatic consequences. It placed limitations on the "flexibility of alignment" of the major powers that interfered with the application of traditional and tested balance-of-power formulas. In France, the dominant expressions of ideology were anti-German nationalism and anti-Communism. Geopolitical factors and the Right-wing composition of the Bloc National–dominated legislature were responsible for the lack in France (in contrast to Britain) of a strong or effective current of Wilsonian idealism and pacifism. Except for the isolated Marxists, there was no principled dissent from these ideological positions; the divisions in the legislative majority that were expressed by the difference between the Briand and Poincaré governments related to the wisdom of according to these almost universally held beliefs a dominant influence on foreign policy decisions. Of the two important ideologies, both of which were defined in negative terms, anticommunism had by far the more dislocating effect on foreign policy. Vehement hostility toward Germany on the part of the Right impeded compromise and cooperation, but it corresponded fairly closely to the alignment of political, strategic, and economic issues in French foreign policy. Anticommunism, however, had the practical effect of a major diplomatic reversal, changing, as it did, the very basis of a security policy against Germany that had proven relatively effective over more than a generation; and it forced France, instead, to rebuild its encirclement policy on the wobbly foundations of the East European states.

Britain did not make the same error. Its revisionist bias toward Germany accorded with its economic needs as well as its interest in creating a Continental balance of power. Hostility toward Soviet Russia, in Britain's case, was not really a departure from the traditional calculation of the national interest. In fact, it was Britain's alliance with Russia that had interrupted a long history of friction, a product of the conflict of imperial ambitions in Asia. Whatever may be thought of the intrinsic wisdom of Britain's ideological position in the early postwar years, it was complementary, rather than contradictory, to the general thrust of the nation's political and security policy. Furthermore, in matters of economics, Britain was pragmatic enough to discard its weighty ideological baggage in the interest of striking a profitable deal.

Ironically, some of the most reactionary elements, in the Western world, represented by the German Right, were inhibited least by their philosophical ideas and prejudices. Germany was at too great a disadvantage vis-à-vis the Western powers to allow such scruples to interfere with an improvement in its political and military relationship with the Soviets. Its military leaders and professional diplomats gradually persuaded democrats and republicans to reach practical, secret military arrangements and to reconcile political and economic differences in the Rapallo Treaty.

The Soviets, themselves, were particularly anxious to come to terms with the European powers. They suffered gravely under their isolation, particularly because their failure to achieve diplomatic recognition, acceptance, or even tolerance, made them ineligible to receive the foreign credits they needed so desperately to rebuild their shattered country. Although they were committed to the establishment of socialism, they certainly were undogmatic in their choice of means. They actively sought trade agreements with the West, and, under the NEP, they made remarkable compromises between their principles and the realities they faced. Their offers on debt compensation, long-term leases for expropriated properties, and trade concessions were not only reasonable under the circumstances, but they appear to have been motivated by a genuine desire to achieve some sort of *modus vivendi* with a hostile environment. Only when the Allies demonstrated the boundlessness of their demands—demands which would have reduced Russia to a virtual economic colony, carved into spheres of influence and powerless to control its fate, by virtue of extraterritorial privileges—did the Russians suspend their initiative.

Rigid ideological attitudes were a luxury for a country in France's position. Like a Proustian *demi-mondaine* whose rhinestone tiara cost the week's food allowance, considerable sacrifice in other areas was necessary to maintain even a spurious approximation of the chosen image. The price of this role playing was lonely isolation, insecurity, and the humiliating need to solicit support from an unsympathetic Britain, which, in a businesslike way, demanded favors in return. Through the independent and defiant mask France presented to the world could be seen the tarnished traces of inner fears and haunting doubts that belied the outward pride. Barely able to fend for itself in the present, France worried about a time when its powers would pale in comparison to those of its competitors. And it was torn between the now glorified and embellished memory of a past when it did not have to compromise and the prospect of a future which dictated an unaccustomed prudence.

France's policy in Eastern Europe was traceable largely to its ideological biases. Almost from the beginning, France's commitments there proved to be more of a liability than an asset, except to those investors who reaped profits from the association. When, in the course of the Russo-Polish war, the Poles had been driven back to Warsaw by a Russian army equipped with more spirit than armaments, the French felt compelled to call upon Britain for what they depicted as the defense of Western Civilization. The British made it clear, though, that they had no real interest in the East European states. Their motivation in aiding France and Poland was to prevent the spread of communism to Germany.

Thus, while France was defending Western Civilization, Britain was defending Germany—or, more precisely, its vision of the Germany required by the British economy. The "barbed wire" policy in Eastern Europe placed France in an overcommitted position to protect states that were intended to encircle Germany and to contain communism but were themselves encircled by hostile and potentially overwhelming powers. Even in the clashes over Upper Silesia, German irregulars had managed to hold their own against the Poles. What help was Poland expected to provide against a rearmed Germany and recovered Russia when it performed so poorly against their most ragged military units? Instead of providing France with the means to pursue an independent policy, the responsibilities to Eastern Europe were a drain that made France even more dependent upon Britain. As Poincaré ultimately made clear to Britain, France's real interest in a guarantee treaty was not to bolster security in the West, where the French were confident Britain would feel compelled, out of self-interest, to participate against a German attack, but to protect France's exposed outposts in the East. This Continental policy, and the extra commitments it made on French power, was paradoxical indeed on the part of a nation that claimed to be insecure within its own borders.

Another consequence of France's ideological orientation was its contribution to the German-Soviet rapprochement at Rapallo. Poincaré's intemperate intransigence and unwillingness to compromise with either of the two states was a major factor contributing to the conclusion of their pact. If this was a deliberate *politique du pire* intended to rally Britain to France's side, it again demonstrated how ideology contributed to dependence upon Britain. If it was merely the product of blunders or an absence of feasible choices due to the limitations of domestic politics, it illustrated how the blinders of ideology interfered with a perception of, or action in accordance with, the national interest. For no leader could show that Rapallo was not contradictory to the aims of French foreign policy without resort to a type of perverseness that had become all too habitual.

Briand came to understand the anomaly of the combination of a thirst for normalcy and a doctrinal stance that put his country out of step with the other major powers. In the half year that followed the Second London Conference, he attempted to resolve the dichotomy between heartfelt hatreds and his perception of *raison d'état*. This meant that he attempted to eliminate first the impediments to a reconciliation with Germany and then those that stood in the way of beneficial relations with the Soviets. But his opponents on the Right pictured him as carried away by his own rhetoric to a land of illusions, while the only realistic policy was one in which France completely satisfied its claims upon these two states.

It is difficult to explain the tenacity of the dominant ideological mold in light of its counterproductive effects. In a correlative manner, however, it should be noted that its short-term consequences for influential minorities were not negative. The majoritarian Right-wing forces that stood most firmly for hostility to Germany and Soviet Russia were a coalition of elites whose economic interests and electoral success were served by expressions of nationalism and anticommunism. The Bloc National had ridden to power on the crest of these sentiments. Its appeal to a widespread electorate, whose economic interests it certainly did not represent accurately, depended largely on the picture it presented of itself as the party of victory in a world that was filled with peril and that was misunderstood by its naive opponents. Among the strongest backers of its Rightist cabinets were those of a military bent who identified with the army's hard-line policy in Eastern Europe and on the Rhine. Disgruntled bondholders and investors whose properties had been confiscated because of the Russian Revolution gathered under the leadership of those who stood most firmly in defense of their creditor positions, not appreciating that this inflexible adherence to the letter of their rights would deprive them of any compensation at all. They were joined by Catholics and others who feared the bolshevization of France. Investors in Poland and Czechoslovakia, including the nation's largest banks and heavy industries, exerted powerful pressures on all French governments in support of the links that brought them profits. Of course it was Briand, not Poincaré, who negotiated the lucrative alliance with Poland. Even when he advocated conciliation toward Russia and Germany, he was careful not to appear to weaken the French ties in Eastern Europe. Many of these same economic forces, however, also were interested in exploring other opportunities. Therefore, Briand's policy of entente with Germany and rapprochement with Russia received the tentative endorsement of this expansion sector of the French business community which expediently built armament factories in Eastern Europe and hedged their investments with support of functional economic cooperation with the enemies of the Eastern European states. Opportunistic, but hardly adventurous, this business sector made its acquiescence contingent upon an overwhelmingly favorable balance of profit and risk. And, when the prospect of a Ruhr occupation under Poincaré came to appear a surer road to their goal than a freely negotiated bargain under Briand, the weight of this group shifted in favor of the former—just as, after the disappointment in the Ruhr, they would return to the policies of the latter. Thus it was not so much that ideological values in France ran deeper than in Britain, but that the opportunist alternative failed to retain the support of the opportunists.

THE INTERRELATIONSHIP OF STRATEGY, ECONOMICS, AND IDEOLOGY

Although questions of security, economics, and ideology can be analyzed individually, to the French policy-maker they hardly were autonomous spheres. Rather, each impinged upon the others in a pattern that circumscribed a range of diplomatic possibilities, but excluded the maximization of values in all areas simultaneously. This was a consequence not only of systemic conditions but also of the prevailing alignment of domestic forces, and of the logical incompatibility of certain choices in one area with contradictory ones in another. The exclusion of a small number of dissenters from participation in power contributed to a broad consensus on basic values. When political rivalries were based on more than personal differences and ambitions, they focused on the means to be adopted in pursuit of shared goals, or upon the relative priority to be accorded to any particular aim. Two tendencies or persuasions were manifested over each of the three major sets of issues: a "hard-line," principled defense of legal rights and prerogatives, and a "soft-line," pragmatic policy of accommodation, conciliation, and opportunism. Because the success of either of these approaches depended upon the construction of a domestic and international constituency, it was difficult to combine a hard-line policy over one issue with a soft-line on another without losing necessary sources of support.

A web of intersecting problems and policies was canopied by an enveloping concept of security. In addition to the narrow definition of military security against German attack, the expansive meaning of security included economic and ideological preferences. Together, these three elements expressed the general nature of the relationship French governments sought to establish with the domestic and international political environments. Economic security comprised the physical reconstruction of France as well as domestic economic recovery and stability. It also included the development of a strong export sector and the growth of heavy industry—especially that part of it important for war production—to a powerful, and preferably dominant, position on the Continent. The final element was the collection of debts: reparations from Germany; bonds and compensation from Soviet Russia. Prophylaxis against contaminating revolutionary ideas and movements from domestic or foreign sources, as well as the prevention of domestic division and turmoil through the preservation of anti-German nationalist unity, were the essence of ideological security. Military security did not only signify a capacity to emerge triumphant in any conceivable conflict. For the French emphasis was placed upon the deterrence of war through economic preparedness, disarmament of Germany, independent military strength, and the weaving of an awesome network of meaningful alliances surrounding a Franco-British entente. Unfortunately for them, however, the French lacked the independent means to impose their vision or to achieve this ultimate expression of national goals without concessions and compromises. In effect, the selection of priorities among these values entailed the abandonment of their simultaneous pursuit and the sacrifice of transforming certain goals into the means to achieve others through a process of negotiation and bargaining with other states. The tragedy of postwar French diplomacy lay in the painful realization that a bloody victory yielded no triumph, much less a world shaped to the needs and desires of the victor. It is hardly surprising that most Frenchmen shrank from acquiescence to the distasteful reality of their postwar dilemma until sobered by repeated setbacks.

France's adjustment to the postwar situation was impeded by domestic division over priorities, policy conflict with other states, and the complexly interrelated and contradictory implications of cherished values. This confusion of countervailing motives and consequences resulted in a stalemate. For example, when France faced the problem of how to provide for its military security, its ideal response was to reinforce the alliance with Britain, to build a strong alliance system, to enforce the disarmament provisions of Versailles, to achieve economic dominance over Germany, partly through reparations, and a less ideological attitude toward economic relations with Russia. France's policy in Eastern Europe, however, entailed a commitment to anti-Soviet and anti-German policies that were difficult to reconcile with Britain's demands, especially given Britain's postwar divorce from the new states it reluctantly had helped to create. There were domestic interests which supported these policies as well as a policy of harshness toward Germany, for economic, ideological, and strategic reasons. Relaxation of ideological attitudes toward Germany and Russia would have confused public opinion and encouraged the spread of revisionist ideas. To opt for one form of increased military security was to abandon elements of economic and ideological security and to sacrifice independence in strategic policy on the Continent.

Similar predicaments were encountered in the attempt to maximize economic and ideological security. German resistance to French reparations claims forced France to choose between a policy of collection in full through threats or the actual use of force and compromise agreements. British opposition to the first of these alternatives carried the sanctions of isolation or denial of the guarantee treaty. Another consequence relevant to French military security was the extent to which severity could be expected to stir German vengeance. Obviously, military occupation would provoke fierce resentment, while a mutually beneficial compromise offered the hope that a climate of functional cooperation might heal broader political differences. But compromise agreements such as Wiesbaden or negotiations for industrial entente ran into British opposition, German bad faith, and a cool domestic reception. The European reconstruction plan altered the nature of the choice France was forced to make without eliminating the necessity to choose between values. For to deal with Russia as with any other power in order to obtain compensation, recover debts, and provide Germany with the means to pay reparations would weaken an ideological position of domestic utility and strengthen the ideological opponents. Thus, it would make nonsense of many aspects of France's strategic policy in Eastern Europe by establishing a precedent and an incentive for rapprochement with a powerful neighbor. Not to deal with the Soviets in a businesslike way would eliminate an important prospect for European economic recovery. It would destroy the chances for partial reimbursement of France's prewar investors and bondholders and the hopes for profitable economic relations on the part of aggressive industries and investors.

Experiences in the first half-year of his ministry in 1921 demonstrated to Briand the impossibility of combining all aspects of French values and the necessity for choice between a hard-line policy of force and an opportunistic policy of accommodation. The second half of Briand's ministry demonstrated to Poincaré the costs of accommodation, both in terms of the sacrifice of values and the failure to maintain a legislative majority. In the beginning of his ministry, therefore, he too opted for a policy of principle which entailed the simultaneous maximization of values, but to no greater avail than his predecessor. In the second half of his tenure, he would shift to a policy of force which, by comparison, made the price of accommodation seem less costly than before, thereby preparing the way for a conciliatory solution.

In terms of its aspirations, French foreign policy was an obvious failure in 1921–1922. The cause of this failure can be traced to the nature of these aspirations, or more precisely to the nature of these aspirations seen in the light of French resources and world conditions. France did not achieve a reasonable relationship between the ends and the means of foreign policy. This left the country in a peculiar quandary: committed beyond its capabilities to serve influential domestic groups or foreign states and yet dependent for its most basic and legitimate security interests upon coordination with the British, whose general outlook diverged markedly from that of the French and who, out of self-interest, obstructed French policies of either force or cooperation. In large part, France's dilemma derived from a schizoid reaction to the outcome of war. The awful toll the war had exacted in lives and property left a portion of French consciousness stunned and pessimistic. Yet participation in the victorious alliance and the very costs of the war also contributed to a mood of intransigence and chauvinism that ignored the tragically ambiguous and indeterminate results of so much carnage. The latter reaction was encouraged by France's leaders as an antidote to deep-seated depression. But the propagation of irresponsible illusions of national prowess only resulted in overconfidence. This attitude stood as an obstacle to compromise in the postwar period and, hence, as a source of the spiraling cycle of disillusionment and defeatism which accompanied France's successive failures.

Illusions of omnipotence and fears of vulnerability formed an incongruous and unstable foundation on which to base the definition of foreign policy objectives. Adjustment to the difficult realities of the postwar world required flexibility, discrimination, and courage on the part of France's leaders. Instead, for the most part, they feebly attempted to reconcile illusions and fears by defining an ideal vision of France's place in Europe as a minimal condition of security. Ideological rigidity and a shortsighted and class-biased view of economic interests were incorporated into an uncompromising definition of security, expressive of this peculiar combination of pessimism and overconfidence. The majority of Frenchmen admired the emperor's new clothes, not wishing to notice the unadorned and embarrassing reality of a less-than-commanding presence.

LOCARNO AND TRANSCENDENCE OF THE
VICTOR-VANQUISHED RELATIONSHIP

It is possible to specify precisely the moment during which the victor-vanquished relationship was transcended following World War I. It occurred on the afternoon of October 8, 1925, in a conversation between the British, French, and German foreign ministers: Austen Chamberlain, Aristide Briand, and Gustav Stresemann. They were gathered at the Locarno Conference to conclude negotiations for a treaty to guarantee the security of the Franco-German border. To understand the significance of their discussion, however, it is necessary to highlight developments following the Cannes and Genoa Conferences.

Often acting at crosspurposes with Britain, France found it impossible to achieve either its defensive or offensive goals regarding Germany and Europe. Early in the postwar period, the French discovered that the peace they desired would not be self-executing. In the costly military occupation of the Ruhr in 1923, France found itself helpless to employ coercion to achieve net benefits. At the same time, attempts to produce conciliation with substantial fulfillment of the treaty through private economic ententes proved futile. Europe required the intervention of the United States to restabilize its dire economic situation with the Dawes Plan of 1924.

The success of the London Conference to implement the Dawes Plan permitted a reconsideration of the problems of European security and Western relationships with Russia. The elections at the end of October 1924, which brought the Conservative party to power in Britain, were a mixed blessing for France. On the one hand, this development meant that France's security concerns would be treated more sympathetically. On the other hand, the election of the strongly anti-Communist Conservatives, whose ascendance owed much to the scandal caused by the notorious Zinoviev letter, occurred precisely when the Herriot government finally extended diplomatic recognition to the Soviet regime. It soon became clear what the new British government meant when it envisaged the security of "Western Europe."[21] In December, Prime Minister Baldwin emphasized to the French ambassador the need for "une étroite coopération franco-anglaise qui, en présence des causes de désordre qui agitent l'Europe, l'Orient et l'islam, doit . . . avoir pour object la défense de notre commune civilisation."[22] The problem was stated even more bluntly in an anonymous memorandum circulated among pro-French members of the British cabinet and leaked to the press. This document characterized

Russia as "the most menacing of our uncertainties," particularly in Asia,[23] and it called for a new Franco-British entente to meet this threat: "it must be in spite of Russia, perhaps even because of Russia, that a policy of security must be framed."[24]

The opportunity to solidify ties with Britain and to normalize its relationship with Germany in the framework of a security guarantee exerted a strong attraction upon France. At the same time, domestic opposition[25] to the recognition of the Soviets and the unhappiness of its allies in Eastern Europe interfered with France's pursuit of a friendly Russian policy. The Soviets, for their part, were aware of the dangers of an anti-Soviet entente between Britain, France, and Germany. Already faced with the hostility of Britain under Conservative leadership, they worked to preserve the advantages of the Rapal combination with Germany and to improve relations with France.

They found a receptive partner in France's new ambassador to Moscow, Jean Herbette. Herbette was a champion of Franco-Russian cooperation for both economic and strategic reasons, and he worked energetically to translate his preferences into policy. As the idea of a Western security treaty materialized and progressed, however, the Quai d'Orsay decided to bridle its enthusiastic envoy. An important memorandum of March 28, 1925,[26] explicitly rejected Herbette's analysis and prescriptions. Contrary to Herbette's expectations, it asserted that a policy of cooperation with Russia could not be reconciled with France's policy in Eastern Europe, particularly in Poland. Furthermore, it anticipated difficulties with London as the result of a rapprochement with Russia and demonstrated special concern over the fate of the security treaty. The document found Russia to be still too unstable and weak to serve as a reliable military replacement for Poland, and Soviet propaganda and revolutionary activities were regarded as potential threats. In economic matters, it advised against being drawn into Russia's game of playing off bondholders against investors: "Ce serait en effet faire le jeu des Russes que de laisser dissocier le passé de l'avenir et opposer les intérêts des nouveaux concessionnaires à ceux des anciens prêteurs." The memorandum saw little need to rush into economic arrangements for political purposes, nor did it find purely economic arguments especially persuasive:

La pénurie de capitaux dont nous souffrons à l'heure actuelle, le caractère aléatoire et probablement peu rémunérateur des placements qui s'offrent à nous en Russie sont autant d'arguments en faveur d'une politique de prudence consistant surtout à surveiller la situation et à voir venir, sans prendre aucun engagement prématuré.

It recommended a similarly cautious attitude in political matters, a stance somewhere between "la politique d'alliance d'avant 1914 et . . . la politique d' encerclement qui a conduit à la guerre de Crimée." But it was clear from the context which attitude the Quai D'Orsay would adopt if forced to choose.[27] The British attitude toward Russia and Soviet attitudes toward a Western pact inevitably gave Locarno the aura of such a choice.

There were important advantages that led Germany's foreign minister to work actively for the conclusion of a guarantee treaty. Foremost among them was Germany's symbolic reinstatement in the international system as an independent actor. With restored status and with increased value to its former enemies, Germany hoped to win concessions on the terms of the peace, especially those regarding military occupation. Diplomatically, Stresemann sought to create a counterbalance to Rapallo and to gain leverage as the balancing factor between East and West. He also sought to gain an acknowledgement of a theoretical distinction between the validity of the Versailles settlement in Western and Eastern Europe, opening the question of peaceful German gains to the east. Not least important were the economic gains which Germany, like France, anticipated would flow from a relaxation of political strains with France. The progress toward Locarno was punctuated and facilitated by progress toward a general Franco-German commercial accord and by optimistic developments in negotiations between private industries.

The treaties signed at Locarno provided for guarantees by Britain and Italy of the border between France and Germany as well as that between Belgium and Germany. Separately, Germany signed treaties of arbitration with France's allies, Poland and Czechoslovakia. These were not guaranteed by Britain or Italy. The significance of Locarno was far broader than indicated by these formal instruments. Informally, understandings were reached on the evacuation of the Cologne occupation zone, on the encouragement of Franco-German economic cooperation, and on Germany's membership in the League of Nations.

It was in discussions relative to the final point that the real nature and meaning of Locarno were revealed. Article 16 of the League Covenent required all members to participate in sanctions against any state designated as an aggressor. Stresemann strongly resisted the implications of this article and asked for a special interpretation. France and Britain refused. Both sides envisioned the possibility of a Russo-Polish conflict in which Germany would be asked to take action or permit French troops to cross Germany to protect Poland. Stresemann's position was that in its disarmed state, Germany could not afford to open itself to the threat of reprisals. In the crucial conversation of October 8, 1925,[28] Briand contended that if Germany sought equal rights it had to assume equal obligations. While he claimed that neither the league itself nor the accords in question at Locarno were directed against Russia, he was skeptical of the meaning of German resistance to this provision, an undisguised reference to the Rapallo combination. Then Briand issued a challenge:

L'Allemagne doit choisir. Elle ne peut avoir à la fois un pied dans la S.D.N. et un pied dans un autre camp. D'ailleurs, si la Russie est animée d'intentions pacifiques, le problème ne se pose pas et les craintes allemandes sont vaines. Si la Russie, au contraire, nourrit des pensées, d'agression, est-il possible que l'Allemagne assiste, les bras croisés, à une lutte qui mettrait en danger la civilisation européenne toute entière?

When Prime Minister Luther again protested, Briand emphasized the potential dangers to Germany of Soviet aggression:

Ce n'est pas une guerre ordinaire, elle apporte avec elle autre chose que des menaces politiques et économiques, les autres membres de la Société deploient tous leurs efforts pour arrêter le péril; cependant, l'Allemagne, qui siège au Conseil, regarde, passive, ce qui se passe et aide, sans le vouloir peut-être, mais néamoins effectivement, l'ennemi commun, car dans certains circonstances ne pas agir, c'est tout dee même agir.

Les Allemends peuvent-ils croire que, parce-qu'ils voudront demeurer neutres la guerre les respectera? Ils la connaîtront au contraire et particulièrement horrible parce que avant même que n'àrrive a leur frontière l'armée qu'ils se seront refusés à combattre, la guerre civile aura éclaté chez eux. C'est alors que l'Allemagne sera vraiment un champ de bataille.

M. Briand ne dit pas que les arguments allemands soient sans force. Il connait toute la valuer de certains raisonnements sentimentaux; mais il faut, en face, placer la réalité, à savoir que ni matériellement, ni moralement l'Allemagne, dans l'hypothèse prévue ne pourrait conserver la position qu'elle déclare vouloir adopter.

Stresemann then focused specifically upon German disarmament:

Le principe du désarmement a été à l'égard de l'Allemagne poussé trop loin. Alors que la propagande bolchéviste prépare une revolution mondiale, les Allies ne voient que les organisations nationalistes en Allemagne; il faut voir aussi les organisations rouges qui, si la guerre éclatait avec la Russie, retiendraient toutes les forces allemandes pour émpecher que des troubles n'éclatent à Dresde à Hambourg ou en Thuringe. La première mesure que devraient prendre le Gouvernement allemand serait de proclamer l'état de siège reinforcé. M. Briand croit-il que dans une telle situation, l'Allemagne pourrait songer à envoyer les troupes au dehors?

Finally, Austen Chamberlain spoke up, citing the case of Finland. Despite its common border with Russia, it did not seek to avoid its obligations under the League Covenant. He reminded Germany that "si l'Allemagne prend part à la lutte, dans ces conditions, elle devient alliée de tous les membres de la Société des Nations." Furthermore, "elle serait assurée de l'appui de tous les membres de la Société; les Etats qui l'ont désarmée seraient les premiers à la réarmer."[29] On this note, the session ended. The victor-vanquished relationship had been transcended, at least in the minds of the Allies.[30]

What was the value to France of this, the high point of the peace? In terms of defensive goals France obtained a legally weak guarantee of its border with Germany, one which many Frenchmen had long argued required no special treaty since its defense wholly conformed to British self-interest. In fact the excessive evenhandedness of Britain's guarantee of both France and Germany was regarded by many Frenchmen as an insult and a symbolic weakening of special ties. In return, France made important concessions on occupation policy, weakened its stand on German disarmament, and accepted a fateful decision regarding the divisibility of the peace, and of German obligations to the West and the East, which undermined its own alliance structure. With respect to offensive goals, Locarno certainly reinforced the economic, class, and ideological interests of British and French elites. It obtained these gains by rewarding cooperative German counterparts. This was the essence of the package deal for transcendence of the victor-vanquished relationship. It is against these fruits of victory, distributed to a few, that the property losses, death, and suffering of millions in World War I must be weighed to obtain a measure of the utility of war, even a victorious one.

NOTES

1. "Total conventional war" refers here to a strategic conflict among relatively equal opponents in which neither side possesses atomic or nuclear weaponry and each is engaged in an effort to mobilize, aggregate, and deploy maximum force.

2. Edward M. Collins, ed., *Karl von Clausewitz: War, Politics, and Power* (Chicago: Gateway, 1962), p. 255.

3. The implicit formulation, Utility = Value minus Cost, is taken from Klaus Knorr, *On the Uses of Military Power in the Nuclear Age* (Princeton: Princeton University Press, 1966), pp. 14–15.

4. The concept and the implications of the "expansion of force" are developed in Robert E. Osgood and Robert W. Tucker, *Force, Order, and Justice* (Baltimore: John Hopkins Press, 1967).

5. The role of defense serves to further distinguish strategic nuclear war from total conventional war. Unlike the most devastating conflicts before atomic weapons, the nature and magnitude of destructive power deliverable over thousands of miles precludes any meaningful defense under today's technological conditions. The most cherished values of a society are openly exposed to the enemy's forces. In conventional warfare, though less so when it is accompanied by intense levels of strategic bombardment, the "hard shell" of the state is largely shielded by its armed forces. (See John Hertz, *International Politics in the Atomic Age*, New York: Columbia University Press, 1959.) This defense is circumvented and rendered useless by a nuclear missile attack from the air, and no innovations in protection have proved sufficiently reliable and inexpensive to reverse this offensive superiority.

In conventional warfare, threats and actions to compel the enemy population to undertake desired behavioral patterns can only be effective once the opposing army has been defeated and the "hard shell" pierced, leaving the soft core of the enemy's population and values vulnerable to escalating increments of pain and suffering. A consequence of the exposure of values to the enemy in a nuclear war is that a situation of coercion is directly and immediately established. Threats combined with escalating increments of destruction or commitment create the basis for "punitive diplomacy" in the very course of a conflict, rather than after its termination (see Thomas C. Schelling, *Arms and Influence*, New Haven: Yale University Press, 1966, esp. pp. 69–91).

6. Lewis Coser, *The Functions of Social Conflict* (New York: Macmillan Free Press, 1964), p. 140.

7. See "National Security as an Ambiguous Symbol," reprinted in Arnold Wolfers, *Discord and Collaboration* (Baltimore: Johns Hopkins Press, 1962, paperback edition), pp. 147–165.

8. It can do the same with respect to competing demands emanating from a single victor.

9. The case of Germany following World War II is an apparent exception. But the effectiveness of occupation policies in Germany was a function of the transcendence of the victor-vanquished relationship, not of its implementation by force. See below.

10. Kenneth Waltz, "The Function of Force," *Journal of International Affairs*, vol. 21, no. 2, 1967, p. 227.

11. The usage of this term corresponds to Stanley Hoffmann's definition in "Obstinate or Obsolete? The Fate of the Nation State and the Case of Western Europe," in Stanley Hoffmann, ed., *Conditions of World Order* (Boston: Houghton Mifflin, 1966), pp. 110–160. It "is made up altogether of a nation-state's internal features . . . and of its position in the world," and consists of "a composite of objective data (inside: social structure and political system; outside: geography, formal commitments) and subjective factors (inside: values, prejudices, opinions, reflexes; outside: one's own traditions and assessments of others, and the other's

attitudes and approaches toward oneself); some of its components are intractable, others flexible and changeable" (p. 116).

12. This phrase is usually attributed to Sigmund Neumann.

13. W. M. Jordan, *Great Britain, France, and the German Problem, 1918-1939* (London: Oxford University Press, 1943).

14. Arnold Wolfers, *Britain and France Between Two Wars* (New York: W. W. Norton and Company, Inc., 1966). This book was originally published in New York by Harcourt, Brace and Company in 1940.

15. Paul Reynaud's speech of December 27, 1935, to the French Chamber; quoted in Wolfers, *Britain and France*, p. 20.

16. This case study is based primarily upon archival research.

17. Passim.

18. Wolfers, *Britain and France*, p. 133.

19. Fear of spillover, in fact was an important reason for the lukewarm attitude of French industry toward Wiesbaden.

20. This does not contradict statements above which suggest that there were good reasons to restore the old anti-German alliance. These reasons were neglected or underrated, and preference was given instead to the policy in Eastern Europe.

21. Archives of the French Ministry of Foreign Affairs (MAE); Sainte-Aulaire; No. 608; November 4, 1924; Z.284.1; Grande Bretagne 40.

22. MAE; Montille; Tel. 731-4; December 11, 1924; Z.284.4; France-Grande Bretagne 57.

23. MAE; "British Policy Considered in Relation to the European Situation"; February 20, 1925; Z.284.6; Grande Bretagne-Sécurité 72.

24. Ibid.

25. In addition to the traditionally anti-Communist groups which expressed disapproval, a new organization, the Ligue Républicain Nationale, was organized by former President Millerand to develop opposition among members of the Right, defeated several months earlier in the elections which brought to power the Cartel des Gauches.

26. MAE; "Politique de la France à l'égard de la Russie; Note pour M. le Président du Conseil", March 28, 1925; p. 53.

27. Later in the year the French position became even sharper as France saw Russia attempt to restrain Germany from participation in a security treaty. France also blamed Russia for stirring rebellion in French colonies, particularly Morocco. See MAE; Berthelot to Herbette; Tel. 223; June 28, 1925; Z.619.17; Russie-Allemagne XIX.

28. See MAE; Berthelot; Tel. 11-21; October 8, 1925; Z.284.6; Grande Bretagne-Sécurité 84 and MAE; "Notes prises par le secrétaire français . . ." October 8, 1925; Z.284.6; Grande Bretagne-Sécurité 85.

29. The parallel with the circumstances surrounding the rearmament of Germany following World War II is obvious.

30. Article 16 was finally regulated by a vague interpretation. Germany was to support League sanctions to an extent compatible with its special situation. In effect, this merely recognized the obvious necessity of winning German cooperation at the time of crisis. Meanwhile the success of Locarno, made possible by this formula, signaled—as it was meant to—a warning to the Soviets. After Locarno, Germany signed a new accord with Russia that reaffirmed the Rapallo Treaty, making it clear that it had no more intention of binding itself exclusively to the West than to the East. The Soviets, however, were not inaccurate in their understanding of Locarno as a British-inspired anti-Soviet maneuver to encircle the Soviet Union. See Royal Institute of International Affairs, *Soviet Documents on Foreign Policy*, vol. 2, 1925-1932 (London: Oxford University Press, 1952), p. 57 for Chicerin's statements to this effect.

Section III

CIVILIAN AND
MILITARY
PERCEPTIONS

ADAM YARMOLINSKY

5
PROFESSIONAL MILITARY PERSPECTIVES ON WAR TERMINATION

If wars could be fought by chessmen, it might be relatively easy to avoid the mutual devastation and the boredom of the end game, and to conclude the match when one side or the other had secured a clear advantage. But wars are still fought by flesh-and-blood human beings, who have to suffer mutilation and often death in pursuit of victory; and their feelings, desires, and attitudes—sometimes the attitudes instilled to make them more effective warriors—can get in the way of neat endings to war. Further, these human beings are organized nowadays into very large bureaucratic structures, and the dynamics of these bureaucracies can prolong the wars for which they are organized.

The thesis of this essay is that a better understanding of the motivations of military men, both as individuals and as bureaucrats, can reduce the likelihood that small wars will be prolonged and expanded into bigger wars—even into the Big War that may be the end of modern civilization— but that military attitudes towards war ending don't make a great deal of difference, and the best way to avoid a prolonged war is not to undertake a short war.

It has never been demonstrated that military men are more bloodthirsty, or even more inured to violence than civilians. In fact, the worst cases of genocide in modern history are generally attributed to civilian populations and to civilian political leadership.

But military men do have at least three characteristics, all of them interrelated, that are relevant to the problem of ending wars. They are accustomed to the idea of completing assigned tasks successfully, they expect duly constituted authority to maintain control of any situation, and they are more familiar with, and therefore more confident about military solutions to political problems than about other kinds of solutions.

Professional soldiers are trained to execute commands without hesitation, and to assume personal responsibility for failure, whatever the actual cause. An American officer's response to instructions is "Can do, sir," and the ritual response to a query about failure to accomplish the instructions is "No excuse, sir." These attitudes are essential in combat duty, when men are called upon to perform tasks that they could quite reasonably reject. And they are an important element in conducting the day-to-day business of any large organization, when extraordinary efforts are frequently required just to keep the system intact and functioning. Difficulties arise when the instructions are based on erroneous facts or judgments, or the failure is based on circumstances beyond the control of the responsible officer. This is not to say that senior officers will not question the instructions of their superiors, military or civilian, or that they will not suggest that the blame, or the reason for failure lies altogether outside the military organization. But it is important that civilian leaders understand the bias in the system towards accepting orders unquestioningly, and assuming (or allocating) personal responsibility for failure.

There is a further and more insidious consequence of these attitudes: they introduce a systematic bias towards confidence in the success of one's mission, which may be quite important for combat leadership, but can be dangerous for staff planning. If there is no excuse for failure, it must be an unlikely as well as an improvident event. And if there is a failure, it is assumed, (or is likely to be assumed) that the school solution was incorrectly applied—not that it was the wrong solution or even that no solution is currently available. The next step, then, is to try the same solution over again, but with more men, more firepower, and more air support. And in an organization as large and as powerful as the United States military establishment there is generally more of everything available, at least to deal with the initial stages of a conflict. Again, civilian leadership may have to raise the question insistently, whether more of the same—even a great deal more—will do the trick.

This first set of attitudes tends to reinforce the second set of attitudes, the expectation that duly constituted authority will maintain control of any situation and vice-versa. The civilian authorities may be asking their military professionals, "Can you accomplish such-and-such a goal?" while the military, because they assume that authority must and will prevail, assume that the question amounts to an instruction: "Tell us what you need to accomplish the goal." Then, when the military call for heroic or even ridiculous measures to achieve the objective they assume they have been directed to achieve, the civilians are understandably annoyed. The civilians may not realize that the military have missed their question, in a typical dialogue of the deaf.

Of course, some apparently unreasonable military responses are based on the quite reasonable military notion that they might as well at least try to satisfy some bureaucratic objective—like restoring previous equipment levels—in pursuit of an impossible military objective. But a good many of the military responses to civilian requests for estimates of requirements to "win" the Vietnam War were based on a military assumption that the civilian authorities, United States and Vietnamese, would do what they had to do to achieve political objectives and would do it successfully, even with very large military operations going on all around them, because one has to assume that authority—that is to say, authority on our side—knows what it is doing and will prevail. If the civilian leadership suspects that continuing military activity may be inconsistent with achievement even of limited political objectives, it will have a hard time convincing the military that such a situation is possible, getting the military to modify their tactics because the military tactics get in the way of political goals. This was a major problem in Vietnam, and it is particularly a problem in any conflict situation where objectives must be scaled down, in the search for a resolution of the conflict short of all-out victory.

The third set of attitudes—greater confidence in military solutions to political problems than in other kinds of solutions—tends also to reinforce the other two. If military solutions are more familiar and more reliable for military men, then contingency plans are likely to reflect assumptions that military measures will be pursued to their logical conclusions. The Joint Chiefs' planning for "surgical air strikes" against the missile sites during the Cuban missile crisis involved so large a number of sorties that the plans were unacceptable to ExCom and the President. But it appears that the number of sorties was based on the assumption that the air strikes would be only a prelude to invasion. Because military solutions tend to be more showy and less expensive (since the large fixed costs have already been paid) than other kinds of solutions, civilian authorities may be bemused by the purely military options, as perhaps they were until the culmination of the missile crisis. And the more confidence one has in military solutions, the harder it is to accept a war ending that falls short of total victory.

Apart from and in addition to the attitudes of individual military men, there is a tendency in the military establishment to make the main business of the day a continuing enterprise, and even a growing one, as in any bureaucracy. If that business is a war, even a small war, the military establishment may gear up for it slowly. Some observers complained that even when the Vietnam War was reaching the stage of greatest involvement of U.S. forces, a number of elements in the military were still operating on a business-as-usual basis. Clearly the U.S. military is not bloodthirsty or eager to get into wars, for whatever reason. But once a war is on, everybody wants to get into the act, for much the same reasons that Cole Porter's heroine declared: "If I'm in town, I want to be the toast of it." The overriding importance of service in Vietnam for professional advancement is well known, as well as the ways in which military needs were sacrificed to "needs of the service" in rotating officers rapidly through command positions, in order to give everybody a turn. Missing out is like sitting on the bench all through the championship game. Again, it is important for civilian leadership to realize that military policies calculated to maximize the opportunity for participation in conflict may not always be consistent with maximum effort to get the war over with.

Understanding the prevalence of these attitudes and tendencies in the military is important for the management of war ending strategies. But it would be dangerously foolish to assume that it is enough to be able to calibrate military advice. Military feelings and beliefs have an impact on political decision-making, including decisions on how to end wars, that must be distinguished from the impact of military counsels, and the impact is felt despite the reticence of military men to express their feelings. Soldiers are flesh and blood, and the United States has been fortunate enough that in the wars we have been engaged in for the last quarter-century they have done almost all the fighting and dying. What happens to American soldiers is a matter of deep concern to all Americans. Many American soldiers are professionals, and today all are volunteers, but they are not mercenaries, nor are they regarded as such either by the American people or by political leaders. Once American forces have been engaged in combat, and American lives have been lost, the bases for ending a war have changed drastically from what they were before the fighting began.

The American public can understand and accept the idea of limited objectives in a war. Since the United States lost its nuclear monopoly, the idea of limited war has been unavoidable. Soldiers are particularly aware of the dangers of overstepping this constraint. As one young officer, asked about the frustrations of limited war in Vietnam, put it: "That's the only kind of war I ever hope to fight."

But limited objectives must be differentiated from limited commitments. The commitment of the American military to the objectives that are set for them goes very deep, especially so when they have already suffered casualties in pursuit of the objective. And the commitment of the American public to an embattled military goes quite deep also. The concern over the prisoner-of-war issue in Vietnam clearly arose from this commitment. There have been occasions, of course, when the military complained, as in Korea, that American civilians at home did not know there was a war on. But the suggestion that the United States has used as much in the way of human resources to achieve a military objective as is appropriate under the circumstances, and that, having failed to achieve the objective with those resources, the United States should withdraw, always meets strong emotional resistance. It is argued (forgetting the War of 1812) that the United States has never lost a war. Or, on a more sophisticated level, as in the 1967 McNaughton memorandum unearthed in the Ellsberg papers, that the United States must maintain its reputation as a "good doctor,"[1] presumably always able to save the patient, or at least to maintain its reputation for perfection in technique.[2]

It may not be possible, even if it were judged to be desirable, for the American public and its leaders, civilian and military, to achieve the kind of objectivity, and the detachment from the fate of its military, that would allow for a decision to commit limited military resources to an objective, and if the forces proved to be inadequate, or the level of casualties unacceptable, calmly and rationally to withdraw. When General MacArthur, on his own say-so, raised the ante on the objectives in Korea, the country, under strong presidential leadership, was able to reject the supposed commitment to the larger objective. But when the objectives are raised in order to protect the commitments (and the commitments then increased in line with the new objectives) as in Vietnam, it is a good deal more difficult for the civilian authorities to back off.

There was a brief time when a kind of euphoria about the limited nature of military commitments pervaded the government and the public. This was shortly after the Kennedy administration came into office, when it explicitly abandoned the outmoded Dulles doctrine of massive retaliation. Instead of the impossible and morally abhorrent idea of using nuclear weapons "at times and places of our own choosing," the new administration adopted a doctrine of flexible response, which comprehended particularly the use of "counterinsurgency" military techniques, at the opposite end of the spectrum from violence resulting from the use of nuclear weapons. If a detachment of Green Berets could go out into the jungle villages and—between helping the villagers with their schools and hospitals—defeat the Communist insurgents in single combat, then the use of military force involved very limited commitments indeed.

But the ideal represented by the Green Berets dissolved very quickly in the morass of Vietnam. And the ideal was one that never really caught on within the military, perhaps because it was too offbeat, perhaps because it was not military enough in a traditional sense, perhaps because it confused the constabulary and the warrior functions. The kind of conflict that Green Berets could engage in, one that could be entered into and broken off so easily, may just have been not serious enough for a military establishment that constituted—and still constitutes—the biggest and strongest institution in the United States if not in the world. This raises a question at least whether an establishment of the size and complexity necessary to meet the major commitments of a great power can also be flexible enough to manage—and to terminate—a small war.

The Green Berets were—and are still—considerably more heroic in the popular imagination than in the eyes of their more somberly-capped fellow soldiers. What makes a hero is a key question in the structure of any profession. So long as physicians and medical students see heroic medicine as open heart surgery and organ transplants, the essential business of preventive medicine and public health will continue to take a poor second place in the delivery of health care. So long as policemen see heroic police work as capturing or killing gunmen in a High Noon kind of shoot-out, crime prevention and salvaging potential criminals will take a poor second place in law enforcement. And so long as soldiers see warfighting as more heroic than war-prevention or war-ending, the constabulary function of the military will take a poor second place. In fact, a fundamental change of attitudes among the military might go a long way to changing attitudes in some civilian police forces, which tend to take the military as their professional model.

The military constabulary function is still an unhappily vague concept which has been much discussed but little defined. Were the Roman legions constabulary? Or the nineteenth-century British army operating on the borders of India? Or General Custer's forces at Little Big Horn? Or, for that matter, the U.S. forces at Wounded Knee? In a world of separate sovereignties, where two sovereignties clash, which side is the policeman?

For our present purposes, we can define a constabulary force as one that considers war both as an interruption of its normal duties and as indication of failure in a system of relations in which it has a significant continuing responsibility. Both elements are important, because a primarily war-oriented force could still realize that wars are exceptions to the normal course, or that it had some peace-keeping responsibilities. In fact there is no black and white distinction between the two functions, particularly in a world where the United States has not been involved in a declared war for thirty years, and the second biggest war of the period was explicitly labeled a "police action."

It seems highly unlikely that the United States military forces, or any other great powers' military forces can, in the foreseeable future, become a true constabulary force. Neither the United States nor other great powers are likely to be called on for contributions of military units for constabulary forces in the limited range of circumstances in which they are called on today. That role still goes to nations like Sweden and Switzerland. When, during the Yom Kippur War, the Soviets suggested a joint U.S.-U.S.S.R. peace-keeping force, the United States responded by declaring a world-wide nuclear alert. It is apparent that the Parliament of Man is still well over the horizon, and such hope as we have for avoiding major conflict depends more on mutual self-restraint on the part of the great powers than on joint policing of conflicts among the lesser powers.

In this situation, military attitudes are more important than military functions. To the extent that the United States military can think of itself as constabulary, it can at least accommodate itself with less difficulty to a decision to end a short conflict because costs have outrun the limits of commitment, even if the original objectives have not been achieved. Once the military has accepted the idea that keeping the peace rather than fighting wars is their primary task, they should be better prepared to accept the consequences of limited commitments as well as limited objectives, if war does break out.

When a policeman is killed in the line of duty, the police force makes extraordinary efforts to find and capture his killer. But even if they are reasonably sure of the identity of the group to which the killer belonged, they do not ordinarily declare all-out war on the gang, with heavy weapons and air support. This kind of behavior is generally out of bounds for the police, not only because of the practical danger to innocent bystanders, but because it is inconsistent with fundamental notions of criminal justice, developed over centuries, in which guilt is personal, and the majesty of the law is such that it need not always have the bigger battalions on its side. Police forces can and sometimes do turn police work into all-out war, as the Los Angeles Police Department did with the Symbionese Liberation Army, but these are rare occasions, and in the aftermath police spokesmen tend to be very much on the defensive. The image of the unarmed British bobby is still a very powerful one in Western society, although it cannot compete in the United States with the television-fostered image of the gun-toting sheriff.

Soldiers, almost by definition, are armed men. Yet thoughtful soldiers cannot help wondering about their future role in a world in which war-fighting is an increasingly limited and dangerous option, at least for major powers.[3] The army of the sixties used to joke about their air force comrades-at-arms as "the silent silo-sitters of the seventies." Now that the seventies have arrived, silent sitting appears to be the order of the day for the army as well—while the navy can at least cruise the oceans, testing its abilities to deal with natural phenomena in a relatively unforgiving environment. The issue arises, particularly in bull sessions among younger officers, whether silent sitting will be enough to occupy them. True, there is an endless amount to learn and to teach the troops. Some favor an expanded program of civic action: involvement in civilian public works, going beyond the civil functions of the Corps of Engineers. Others suggest expanded training programs for allies and potential allies.

Until this ferment of debate settles down, U.S. involvement even in a small war could attract professional energies in a way that might make it difficult to disengage. At that point, talk of gradual shift to constabulary functions might be abruptly halted. If, on the other hand, the military has found new satisfying peacetime occupations consistent with its own ideas about what it ought to be and do, it should be able to handle a small military engagement without getting stuck in the process of disengagement.

Much depends, of course, on how the public and the political leadership sees the military in its new role. In the last analysis, it is public attitudes towards the military, rather than the attitudes of the military themselves that have a decisive influence on the process of war-ending for the United States. If the military are regarded, in Albert Biderman's phrase, as "the guardians of our most sacred values," then any assignment that they take on acquires symbolic as well as practical significance; like other rituals, it creates an emotional need among its observers for it to be carried through to its traditional conclusion. If, on the other hand, the military are seen as one of several kinds of valued public servants, a more pragmatic approach to the completion of their appointed tasks may be acceptable to the general public—and therefore to its leadership. When the local fire department makes a judgment in a major fire that it is better to allow the fire to burn itself out rather than risk additional resources—and lives—in continuing to fight the fire, even if lives have been lost in the first stages of fire-fighting, the public reaction is not complicated by a feeling that it is somehow dishonorable to abandon the effort before the fire is completely out.

Being able to calibrate military advice, and to discount it at the appropriate rate, may produce a more realistic view of what needs to be and what can be done to achieve a minimally satisfactory war ending with the resources that are reasonably available, and within even a time-limit that the country will be willing to accept. But knowing when it is time to stop is not the same as having the courage to stop. It is simply not true that Lyndon Johnson and his principal civilian advisors (with perhaps one exception) had an unreasonably optimistic view, based on military advice, of the prospects for achieving their military objectives. They knew how bleak the situation really was. But they were not prepared to run the gauntlet of domestic civilian reactions to withdrawal without achieving the declared objectives. They saw no way of "winning," yet they were not ready to admit that they had fallen short—and they were not willing to face the domestic political consequences. The same unwillingness persisted through the first Nixon administration, and it is not unfair to suggest that it was at least in the air in the four previous administrations that had to deal with Southeast Asia in the twenty years after the end of World War II.

Understanding and modifying military attitudes—and civilian attitudes towards the military—can help to end wars that might otherwise drag out in unnecessary agony, as the war in Vietnam did. But ending wars, like beginning them, is primarily and ultimately the responsibility of civilian political leadership.

NOTES

1. *The Pentagon Papers* (Gravel Edition), vol. 3, p. 604, Beacon Press, Boston, 1971.

2. It is interesting that in a recent survey of officer opinion conducted by Bruce Russett and Raoul Alcala, to the question "Which one of the following considerations do you regard as most important in the formulation of your opinion [on whether the United States should have sent ground troops into Vietnam]?" the most popular response (32 percent) was "consequences for U.S. image as ally." Communication to the author from Raoul H. Alcala, April 12, 1975.

3. In the same survey of officer opinion referred to above, more than 30 percent of the respondents agreed "strongly" or "with qualifications" with the proposition that "ground combat is no longer an effective means of settling disputes."

ROBERT JAY LIFTON

6

THE POSTWAR WAR

My title is ambiguous and has at least two levels of meaning. One is the literal fact that the war goes on, and with active American participation. But the postwar war is that of consciousness, the struggle over the residual meaning of the Vietnam War as perceived by antagonistic groups in American society. I want to discuss contending expressions of survival that can be looked at rather systematically, though they have implications that are enormous and at times unmanageable, both intellectually and politically.

The imagery around which one "survives" a war has much to do with the way in which one fights it and ends it. The surviver imagery begins to take shape long before the war itself is over. In my study of Vietnam veterans I try to show how extreme and immediate feelings of grief and loss, following the deaths of buddies, have a direct bearing on the commission of such atrocities as My Lai: The only way to justify one's own survival is to render that death "significant" by "getting back at the enemy," and if one is unable to engage him in the manner desired, to create an "enemy" out of defenseless peasants. In an "atrocity-producing situation" like Vietnam, where battle lines were obscure and the enemy elusive, survivor imagery actively shaped the quality of the war experience and served to internalize the need for constant atrocities among GI's.

Survivor imagery around wars is self-perpetuating, as is evident, for instance, in the influences of World War I upon World War II. This influence is clear in the powerful effect of Verdun on France's behavior in World War II, with Marshal Pétain, the "hero" of Verdun who had been appalled by the incredible slaughter showing little inclination to assert himself militarily in World War II; as well as in Germany's rearmament and chauvinistic demands for revenge for her humiliation and "betrayal" at Versailles.

In my work in Hiroshima around the experience of the survivor I tried to delineate a general pattern that seemed consistent for virtually all survivors of actual or metaphorical death immersions. The psychology of the survivor has to do with five patterns of response. First is the "death imprint," the impact of death and of one's loss of a sense of invulnerability. The death imprint is associated with emotions organized around what becomes an "indelible image" or set of images. Second, the issue of death guilt, the classical question of the survivor: why did he or she die while I remained alive? The guilt is often focused around various things one felt one had to do in order to survive, around choices one had to make at the expense of others. The third pattern I call psychic numbing or desensitization, loss of feeling in order to escape the impact of unacceptable images. This numbing, necessary at the time, can later give rise to despair, depression, and withdrawal. The fourth pattern has to do with a suspicion of the counterfeit in all relationships, and accompanying anger and rage at one's dependency. Finally, the overall struggle of the survivor is to give form, significance, and meaning to the death immersion, in order to move forward in one's post-holocaust existence.

With that overview of the psychology of the survivor as a background I want to describe three scenes. The first is a White House evening in which the President hosted most of the returning POWs. Irving Berlin was there to lead the singing of "God Bless America." Bob Hope's wife recited a prayer. In the speech he delivered that night the President made the most belligerent defense he had made of his international and domestic programs and of his conduct in association with the Watergate scandal. He issued, in effect, a call to reactivate the deadly romance of war, and to salvage, insofar as that was possible, the synthetic romance of the Vietnam War. The POWs were being used as the center of that call to rally the nation around a sense of immortalizing glory (and of course around Mr. Nixon himself)—all within the lowest common denominator of narrowly conventional nationalism.

The other two scenes suggest the contrast between the peace demonstrations of 1945 and 1973, as flashed on the television screen. One is the night of V-E Day in Times Square, film clips of pure mass joy—which I know to be authentic because I was there in that crowd, a happy nineteen-year-old medical student. The second, Times Square after the 1973 cease-fire—the area itself now looking seedy, almost deserted, a few Vietnam veterans gathered in anger, some drinking, others apparently on drugs, most simply enraged, screaming at the camera, at the society, about having been deceived by the war and ignored upon coming back, one especially enraged black veteran shouting, "You can tell that bastard the war isn't over!"

Those three scenes suggest some of the survivor imagery now having an impact in American life. In thinking about the POWs one must begin with the assumption that, even prior to their being received by the Pentagon and the Administration, they have the survivor's need to try to give significance to their death immersion, which in this case is twofold —that of the war itself, and that of their period of imprisonment in Vietnam. The survivor formulation for these men involves the struggle to find meaning and significance in those lost years (up to seven years for some of them), and to convince themselves and the country that there was some redeeming value in that experience. One way of claiming honor is to call forth the traditional definition of the socialized warrior within which honor consists of standing up under pressures of imprisonment. This approach has been very much emphasized, partly because many in this group received their Air Force training after the general demoralization of American POWs during the Korean War by means of Chinese Communist thought-reform programs.

I would stress not only the struggle of the POWs toward achieving significance and honor in their way of formulating their experience but also the survivor mission which many of them have assumed: that of restoring national honor and pride in relation to some kind of positive feeling about America's contribution in Vietnam. Once one has said this about the survivor struggle of these men themselves, one must immediately emphasize the enormous embrace, orchestration, and manipulation of that kind of imagery by the Nixon Administration for political purposes. The result is that the POWs have been made into instant heroes. This is probably the first war in human history in which the returning prisoners of war have been the national heroes of that war, which in turn has to do with the absolute absence of American heroes in the Vietnam War. This survivor imagery around the POWs becomes inseparable from an insistence that we learn nothing from the Vietnam War and simply return to the simple-minded glorification of the American version of the warrior ethos.

At the opposite pole are the anti-war veterans whom I've been working with for two and a half years in rap groups in New York. My work with these veterans has been both political and psychological. The overall approach of the work has been one of advocacy investigation, in which one holds to certain ethical and political commitments and at the same time tries to attain an approximation to truth through intellectual rigor— using one's own commitments to deepen one's understanding.

The anti-war veterans seek their survivor formulation by expressing the very absurdity of their war. They find meaning in revealing its meaninglessness. Their survivor mission becomes that of telling the truth about the war as they perceived it, no matter how unacceptable that truth is to the American people. As a grassroots effort by veterans of a war to oppose their war while it is still being fought, they are unique in American history.

Part of the truth as these men see it and part of the message they seek to convey is an understanding of the American presence in Vietnam as an atrocity-producing situation. Atrocity was the norm, with My Lai on a larger scale than most other occurrences, but not otherwise exceptional. I spent ten hours interviewing a man who had been at My Lai but had not fired, exploring with him the factors in his past life that had enabled him to refrain from firing. The restraint this man showed was even more impressive, in that he not only refrained from firing but did not pretend to fire (as was the case with a few others in the company, fearful as they were of group disapproval).

There were several elements in the life of this survivor of the My Lai atrocity that seemed important in explaining his refusal to fire and his capacity to risk ostracism from the group. Though this man had broken away from his Catholic teachings in a formal religious sense he retained from it certain imagery about limits beyond which one cannot go. He had grown up a loner, mostly off by himself, living by the ocean, not as a part of childhood groups, and was consequently less susceptible than most to group influence. Finally, he had loved the military and had embraced it strongly after a somewhat confused early adult life. He had excelled in various training exercises, had planned to make the military his career, but had been appalled when he got to Vietnam at the violation of what he considered to be military honor. From the beginning this exceptionally skillful soldier had been "maladapted" to the combat situation in Vietnam.

Guilt is very much part of the survivor imagery of the anti-war veterans. Not guilt of the *mea culpa* kind, but rather what I call animating guilt, which becomes a vital part of the energy for transformation. One recognizes what one has done and takes responsibility for it. The guilt leads to a sense of responsibility, and these men demand that their countrymen expose themselves to guilt and above all to the responsibility for what we Americans have done and are doing in Indochina.

Anger and rage have also been very central to this survivor imagery. And we "professionals" who were in the rap groups with the veterans did not see ourselves as serving a cooling function, but rather as exploring with the veterans the roots of anger and rage. We had plenty of anger and rage of our own about the war and our own related experiences, and we had our own difficulties in redirecting and using that anger. For the veterans, expressing anger and rage could be a way of dealing with violent impulses which they retained from Vietnam and the post-Vietnam experience.

The veterans' survivor formulation also includes a fundamental political critique of spiritual authority in the society. Among the most passionate targets of bitterness and rage in the rap groups were two groups representing that authority: chaplains and "shrinks." Often when these men had been in combat over a period of time they reached a point in which there was a combination of moral revulsion and psychological suffering, which were difficult to distinguish. In seeking some kind of spiritual guidance they were taken to a chaplain or a psychiatrist who would then serve the military function of "helping" the men adjust to combat and to the daily commission of atrocities. The men felt that it was one thing to be ordered by command to commit atrocities on an everyday basis in Vietnam but another to have the spiritual authorities of one's society rationalize and attempt to justify and legitimize that kind of process. They felt it to be a kind of ultimate corruption of the spirit. In sharing in this exploration with them I was led to questions about my profession, about the relationship of psychiatry to the authorities it serves, and about issues concerning professionalism in general.

There is a struggle, in this survivor imagery, against what the veterans call "the John Wayne thing." That really means various forms of supermasculine bravado around war and war-making in attitudes toward each other, and in relationships with women. Probably as much time was taken in discussing this issue of the John Wayne thing as any other subject all through the two-and-a-half years of the rap groups. The John Wayne thing is not without its appeal—for instance, in its stress on absolute loyalty to one's group, which is so prominent in the survivor imagery around POWs. You stay loyal to your group and to your country and you behave bravely, or at least as well as you can, under duress. The men struggle with these issues of maleness very critically and not without difficulty and ambivalence.

Another part of the survivor imagery involves struggling against the gook syndrome—victimization and the need to victimize others. One of the most poignant moments in the rap groups came with a showing of slides of the Vietnamese people, in response to which profound sources of guilt could be tapped. The men recognized that what they called "becoming human again" required rehumanization of their imagery of the Vietnamese.

In this whole process and in their survivor imagery the men connect with analogous groups in American society involved in various critical and experimental pursuits sometimes in connection with those amorphous entities we call youth culture or counterculture. The men seek animating personal and institutional arrangements and attempt to make contact with other currents critical of the society, which can further a general vision of transformation.

In general I saw the transformation that took place around the survivor imagery as having three fundamental stages. The first stage was confrontation, and that meant confrontation with death in Vietnam. The second stage was reordering. That has to do with struggles similar to those people experience in therapy or any meaningful individual change, in which issues of guilt are dealt with and redirected. The third stage is renewal, a new sense of self—and is likely to include the rediscovery of play. The new sense of self is both introspective and extrospective: the men look out at the world in new ways as they reorder their inner imagery as well.

It probably has to be said that most veterans and most Americans are somewhere in-between on that survivor continuum represented by the POWs at one pole and the anti-war veterans at the other. Most Americans, veterans and others, identify with much that the anti-war veterans say about the absurdity of the war. They can also identify with the overall sense of betrayal—with the idea of having been, as the men say, "fucked over" by the war. The war has had no satisfactory resolution for anyone. Still, many cringe at the full message of grotesquery these men bring back. I spoke with a triple amputee who testified before a Senate subcommittee very movingly about the difficulties of getting adequate medical treatment. In addition to everything else this man had suffered he spoke of the doubt he and others had that the experience was "worth it," the feeling that a small minority of Americans underwent a sacrifice that was neither meaningful nor shared. As I spoke with this man he told me of his plans to run for political office in the deep South. I asked him if a dissident like himself could hope to be elected in his state. And he replied, "I'm no dissident. I've got to believe there was some value in that war." That little dialogue taught me a great deal. Here was a man who was deeply impressed with the absurdity of the whole enterprise but had lost so much that he had a strong need to believe there was some value in what he had done. That is a feeling that I think connects with the responses of many Americans, both veterans and the general population.

In general the POWs are an elite military officer group, and the anti-war veterans are mainly enlisted men. Most Americans sense that the heroic image being created around the POWs is at best fragile and is artificially imposed. As more and more conflicts are revealed in the POWs it becomes increasingly possible to see them as simply human—men subjected to a difficult ordeal in a war devoid of American glory—and hardly the kind of heroes the Administration has tried to create of them.

I had the experience of talking with a group of anti-war veterans whom I knew quite well in New Haven just a few days after the cease-fire. They called immediately after the cease-fire and wanted to meet because, as one of them put it, "the guys are having some pretty strong reactions." When I got to see them it was very clear that their main reaction was rage. As they spoke about their responses they told of having dreams recalling deaths of buddies in Vietnam or of horrible deaths of Vietnamese. They also expressed a desire to smash into something or just to take off, the sort of rage that became almost uncontrollable. One of them said, "There's no sense of an ending. A war or anything else has to have a beginning, a middle, and an end. This is a false ending." And he connected that with what he called "the incredible reluctance of the country to face what did go on out there."

These veterans also commented on how much the country seemed to need heroes and how strongly the country was beginning to focus on the POWs. And one of them said, "I'm withholding sympathy for them." He did have a certain amount of sympathy because he felt some affinity with the POWs, who were veterans too. But he saw quite clearly the manipulative manner in which the POWs had been used all through the war as a rationalization for continuing it.

Some of these veterans had tried to celebrate at the announcement of the cease-fire, but their hearts hadn't been in it. They had gone home from the bar early. Lyndon Johnson had died just before the cease-fire, and that had had an impact on them as well. As one of them said, "We had to realize it wasn't just him. It was the whole country." But that realization left them with "no place to put the rage." The men were especially embittered by the phrase "peace with honor." Their sense was that the phrase was being used with complete hypocrisy while the war continued in Laos and Cambodia, while there were still new body counts about the last man to die before the accords and the last man to die after the accords. It was all like baseball statistics, as they put it. And as one said very simply, "It isn't peace and there's no honor."

The men were also worried about what their own identities would be after the cease-fire. One of them said, "We're no longer dissidents against the war, we're just hippies." They were concerned with losing their stature as *veteran*-dissidents. What they were really talking about, I think, was the government's effort at official termination of their own special survivor mission as anti-war veterans. In other words, their survivor mission required that they confront the war and the government's mode of making peace—ostensibly peace with honor, but actually peace with refusal to look at what the war has been for this country and for Vietnam. They regarded the cease-fire agreements as in fact a way of shutting out the possibility of illumination and of a new beginning for the country. One veteran said, "Once and for all it closed the door." And we must keep in mind how much a suvivor in either the POW or anti-war veteran group depends upon the reactions of the country for the activation and encouragement of his own survivor mission and his own well-being within that mission.

But the door isn't entirely closed in all this, and the struggle goes on. One can see that struggle continuing as VVAW changes its name to VVAW/Winter Soldier Organization. The organization is attempting to retain the rather moving imagery that was initiated during the Revolutionary War, when the Winter Soldiers were those who stayed on through the cold and harsh climate, as opposed to the summer soldiers, who drifted away when the going got rough. And, of course, that means staying Winter Soldiers in the struggle for change and against war.

One can see the struggle over consciousness—these competing survivor images—being expressed in two additional ways: the rather crude but basic psychological level having to do with the capacity of the country to confront its own corpses; and in relation to the issue of amnesty. On the matter of confronting the corpses, I want to read a passage written by a sensitive physician named Ronald Glasser in a book called *365 Days*.

Glasser quotes the instructions given by the military to those who are to accompany bodies at funerals:

Each body in its casket is at all times to have a body escort. An effort has been made to find an escort whose personal involvement with the deceased or presence with the family of the deceased will be of comfort and aid. Your mission as a body escort is as follows: to make sure the body is afforded at all times the respect to a fallen soldier of the United States Army. Specifically as follows: To check the tags on the casket at every point of departure. To insist that the tags indicate the remains as nonviewable—that the relatives not view the body. Remember that nonviewable means exactly that—nonviewable.

In commenting on these official instructions to body escorts one could, if one wanted to be sympathetic to the military's task, say that they are being sensitive to the emotions of the next of kin and relatives, for whom seeing bodies, some of them totally dismembered and mutilated, would be more than they could psychologically bear. And I think that's true. But on the more symbolic level these instructions reinforce the impulse in civilian society and the specific pressure of the Administration towards keeping those corpses "nonviewable," against taking a hard look at what we have done in Vietnam whether the corpses in question are our own or those of the Vietnamese. And in that metaphorical sense, our way of ending our Vietnam War raises the large question of the extent to which any country is capable of looking at its corpses in connection with its survivor imagery of that war.

The issue of amnesty also raises the question of the country's consciousness in response to its own survival of the war. Amnesty has enormous significance not only for the 100,000 or so young people numbered among the resisters and exiles but also for a far larger group, a group numbering closer to half a million if one includes deserters and all those who have received less than honorable discharges. The word *amnesty* itself has roots that connect it with forgetting, with amnesia. And indeed while much of the country is all too willing to forget what has been done in Vietnam, there seems to be very little chance that the acts of those who opposed the war will be "forgotten" so that they can freely reenter society. Were amnesty to be granted to these groups, it would be very much a "confirmation" in Buber's sense—an acknowledgment of the moral value of having resisted the war. Agnew and others who have opposed amnesty most bitterly and vituperatively understand this and have said so in simple words: "It would mean that we were wrong and they were right." And the granting of amnesty would be very much a confirmation of the survivor mission of the anti-war veterans.

I would like to return now to the first scene I suggested to you, that of the President in the White House receiving the POWs. It was a beleaguered president who welcomed the prisoners of war, upon whom he was depending so heavily. You recall that on that occasion the President was reacting to the blows around the Watergate scandal, which seemed each day to implicate him further in an unprecedented expression of executive corruption and law-breaking. In response to all this the President called forth the POWs' simple patriotism and made his famous statement to the effect that it was high time we stopped making heroes out of those who steal government documents and publish them in the newspapers. In this the President seemed to be making reference to Daniel Ellsberg, but also—as Ellsberg quite rightly pointed out a few days later—to Nixon's own former assistant, John Dean, who had done something of the same kind.

I want to suggest that not only was the President calling forth simplistic patriotism around the first set of survivor images, that of the POWs, but that Watergate itself has great psychological resemblance to My Lai. The resemblance is of course not literal, but rather in the cast of mind that impelled this sort of process. My Lai occurred in 1968 when the former Administration was in power, not with the same men that brought us Watergate. But it may be that the patterns involved are deeper in American life and less dependent upon the idiosyncracies of particular administrations than one would like to believe. The analogies between the two events are striking. In both cases one can speak of atrocity. At My Lai the atrocity involved the killing of noncombatants on a large scale. At Watergate it involved subverting the electoral process—an atrocity of its own—in a way that makes more likely the kind of military atrocity that occurred at My Lai. In both cases those who carried out the atrocity—the GI's at My Lai, the team mostly of Cubans at Watergate—were in an in-between psychological area between following orders and some sort of internalized impulse toward carrying through their action. In both cases there was a commitment on the part of those involved to carry through the action on behalf of a higher purpose. Neither group was simply following orders; each had, to a degree, a sense of mission.

In both My Lai and Watergate there was enormous manipulation from above and a combination of a strange American capacity to maintain intense idealism and equally intense cynicism. If one thinks, for instance, of a figure like Haldeman in the President's office one senses in him an intense ideological vision of a right-wing kind as well as a fairly pragmatic cynicism in the machinations he is willing to undertake in order to maintain that idealistic vision. One sees in this the kind of totalism that I have discussed in earlier studies. But here I would say what was common to those at high levels responsible for My Lai and Watergate is the absolute requirement—reaffirmed by both recent presidents—that America remain the strongest country in the world. That commitment is to immortalizing American hegemony and to being the dominant world power. One sees in both Watergate and My Lai the simplistic polarization of American virtue and absolute Communist depravity. In the Watergate episode the notion of Communist depravity was extended to include protesters—among whom were anti-war veterans, who were viewed as potentially violent disrupters of the Republican convention. It was around this image of the barbarians at the gates (and this was a real image for those who carried out the Watergate plans) that the "idealism" and sense of mission required were established and internalized.

There is a self-perpetuating quality around the whole Watergate style. One has to keep on doing more things to prevent a recognition of what one has done from reaching oneself or others. So also in My Lai, where atrocity begets atrocity. And in both cases there is an elaborate cover-up which is as serious as the event itself in that it reveals the depth of corruption and corruptibility within existing institutions. One is also struck by the centrality of illusions in both My Lai and Watergate. At My Lai, the illusion was that they had finally engaged the enemy and had gotten him to stand up and fight in an ennobling combat, while in fact the "enemy" was entirely composed of noncombatants. Similarly, at Watergate there was the illusion of ennobling activity around "national security," however dirty the immediate actions—again a "higher purpose."

These illusions are an expression of struggle around consciousness, and indeed there is a counterinsurgency element to both My Lai and Watergate. The difference is that we have moved from the Vietnamese to American protesters, the Democratic party, and indeed most of the American people, who are now being "Vietnamized"—who have to be brutalized, bugged, and manipulated by behind-the-scenes arrangements. Broadly speaking one could say that there is a pattern in which Watergate and My Lai represent desperate last-ditch efforts to maintain a faltering cosmology around the American secular religion of nationalism, which is inwardly perceived to be collapsing. At such a moment, as many people (including Hannah Arendt) have said, there is a greater likelihood of violence or extreme measures of one kind or another—of the kind we have seen at Watergate and My Lai.

The ultimate test of this struggle over consciousness—and I hope I have sketched in enough to make the contending forms of consciousness clear—will be in the answers to the kinds of questions that are always asked after wars and that are going to be asked of us whether today, tomorrow, or in ten, twenty or thirty years: "Daddy, what did you do in the great Vietnam War?" The traditional answer to this question, and the answer which all the manipulation around the POWs seeks to preserve is a simple one: "I fought bravely at Khe Sanh or in the Delta." But the answer that would be given within the new consciousness that the anti-war veterans are seeking to bring into being would be different: "I opposed the war," or "I resisted it," or "I went to prison, or into exile, or in one way or another avoided fighting it," or "I started to fight it and then fled," or "I fought the war and then returned to tell the country the truth." I think that more and more daddies (and, in symbolic ways, mothers too) are beginning to be able to answer the question in terms like those.

But the struggle goes on. And one has to say that in this kind of struggle over consciousness there is no such thing as absolute virtue or purity; it is not to be achieved and I am not even sure it is to be desired. I close with two lines of poetry because I think poetry expresses most clearly this kind of struggle and the difficulties in it. It is a poem called "The Young and the Old," by Richard Eberhart, and the two lines are:

We are easy riders to the fields of grace
A bomb shell in the gut.

Section IV

HONOR AND MORALITY

7
ENDING WITH HONOR

When President Nixon began to speak of ending our involvement in the Vietnam War "with honor" a few years ago, some of us wondered what the concept meant for him. In recent times the idea of honor has taken on an archaic tone; its content has become hazy and ill-understood, curiously unmodern. We have come to associate honor with sportsmanship and with academic codes of proper deportment on examinations and the granting of higher degrees *honoris causa*. In military circles and schools the word has a wider range of application, denoting proper conduct toward one's superiors, equals, and inferiors, and toward the other sex. There is still an honorable discharge from military service, a dishonorable one, and recently one that is neither honorable nor dishonorable, adding to popular confusion about its sense. In checking through reference books like the *Reader's Guide* and the *Philosopher's Index* I find hardly a single reference to honor, which strengthens the impression that contemporary authors in the United States consider it atavistic, harking back to outlived epochs, lingering only in highly conservative institutions today.

Yet it is evident that we cannot do without the principles of honor in any organized society, however various the tokens of honor may be at a given time and however diverse the things that are honored from one society to another. The reason is that honor plays a major role in maintaining social order because it sets up boundaries, establishes hierarchies, and provides individuals with guidance on the kinds of conduct to be valued and the kinds to be disvalued. Honor is ascribed to men by other men and thus requires bearers, bestowers, and observers. Without some idea of what a group considers to be excellent, individuals in the group are deprived of any authoritative guidance for goals worth striving for. Some of our confusion about honor today is a consequence of the loss of authority, about which we hear so much. In any event it seems clear to me that honor as an individual and social value and as a standard for evaluation of others is a universal principle. Thus it cannot be outdated, only neglected; and neglect in thinking about principles in a rapidly changing time like ours is itself a great source of confusion.

Historically we of the Western world are inheritors of a dual concept of honor, very roughly corresponding to our Classical and our Christian heritages. In Homer and the early Greeks, dominated as they were by a warrior ethos, honor was an aristocratic sentiment, the homage demanded by men of superior social rank, excellence in fighting, and leadership, and paid to them by those not possessing these qualities. Its counterpart was shame. When a hero like Hector or Achilles was shamed by his failure to carry through a project of leadership in war, the one alternative left was to die on the field of battle. Life without honor for such men was intolerable. Their reputation with their fellows and with posterity meant everything. Honor was not only "the greatest of external goods," as Aristotle was later to call it, it was the highest good, in the absence of which all others lost their value.

Aristotle himself placed a high valuation on honor. As the thinker who sums up in the most balanced way the ethos of his culture, he defines honor as "the token of a man's being famous for doing good. It is chiefly and most properly paid to those who have already done good; but also to the man who can do good in future. Doing good refers either to the preservation of life and the means of life, or to wealth, or to some other of the good things which it is hard to get either always or at that particular place or time" (*Rhetoric* 1361a).

But Aristotle's teacher, Plato, and Plato's teacher, Socrates, did not estimate honor so highly as did their fellow Greeks. As one of the worldly goods, honor as reputation ranked far below the inner feeling of moral rightness, integrity, and attunement with the gods as cosmic powers. Socrates put this inner interpretation of honor perhaps most eloquently on the occasion of his trial for impiety and corrupting the youth, when he told the jury:

Men of Athens, I honor and love you, but I shall obey God rather than you, and while I have life and strength I shall never cease from the practice and teaching of philosophy . . .

(Apology 29d)

With the Stoics and Christianity, the devaluation of reputation as pride of station, of wealth, of inherited status and other forms of honor went to greater extremes than in Socrates and Plato. With them honor meant honesty, truthfulness, purity of heart, and complete disregard for public opinion. Marcus Aurelius spoke with scorn of honor as a clapping of hands and a clapping of tongues. The one thing that ought to concern a man was "thoughts just, and acts social, and words which never lie, and a disposition which gladly accepts all that happens, as necessary, as usual, as flowing from a principle and source of the same kind" (*Meditations*, Book IV, Section 33). To be honored by God was for the Christian ascetics the only goal, and this often implied to be dishonored and despised by men. The followers of Saint Francis of Assisi "sought shame and contempt, out of love to Christ, rather than the honors of the world, the respect and praise of men. Indeed, they rejoiced to be despised, and were grieved to be honored" (*The Little Flowers of St. Francis*, chapter five). Even when not so extreme as this, the concept of honor became with the advent of Christianity ambivalent, depending essentially on how highly man and all his works were regarded in comparison with the importance of God's gift of eternal life.

Such ambivalence reached a peak in the period of the Renaissance, when the revival of the Greco-Roman culture came as a challenge to established Christian values. I shall resist the temptation to cite much Shakespeare, in whom one sees most poignantly the conflict of this external and inner conception of honor. In his characters there exists the widest range of valuation of honor, from Mowbray in Richard II, who cries out:

> The purest treasure mortal times afford
> Is spotless reputation—that away,
> Men are but gilded loam, or painted clay . . .
> Mine honor is my life, both grow in one;
> Take honor from me, and my life is done: . . .

to a despairing Hamlet, who finds honor like all other uses of the world "weary, stale, flat and unprofitable," to a skeptical Falstaff, who denounces it: "What is honor? A word. What is that word honor? Air. A trim reckoning! Who hath it? He that died a Wednesday. Doth he feel it? No. Doth he hear it? No. Tis insensible then? Yea, to the dead, But will it not live with the living? No. Why? Detraction will not suffer it. Therefore I'll none of it. Honor is a mere scutcheon—and so ends my catechism" (*Henry IV*, Part I, V, 1).

With the philosopher Thomas Hobbes, the Renaissance ambiguity and ambivalence inherent in the idea of honor disappears. With him it takes on a meaning narrowly political and independent of moral and social excellence:

Honorable is whatsoever possession, action, or quality, is an argument and sign of power. And therefore to be honored, loved, or feared of many, is honorable; as arguments of power . . . Nor does it alter the case of honor, whether an action, so be it great and difficult, and consequently a sign of much power, be just or unjust: for honor consisteth only in the opinion of power.

As evidence for his view that honor is unconnected with moral worth Hobbes cites the ancient Greeks, who honored their gods "even though they raped, plundered and killed" (Leviathan, Chapter 10).

But Hobbes's materialistic conception of honor as having to do with external valuation only is a one-sided and as much an extreme in Western tradition as the opposite view of the idealist philosopher Johann Gottlieb Fichte, who once wrote of honor as follows:

There is one thing that counts for me above everything and to which I subordinate all else, from the assertion of which I will not let myself be restrained by any possible consequence, a thing for which I would sacrifice without hesitation my entire earthly well-being, my good reputation, my life, the whole welfare of the cosmos in case it could come in conflict therewith. I call this one thing: *honor*. In no way do I place this honor in the judgment of others concerning my deeds, not even if that judgment were unanimous among my contemporaries and among posterity: On the contrary, it is solely my own judgment of those deeds that can possibly matter.

> (J. G. Fichtes Leben und literarische Briefwechsel, Leipzig, 1862, II, p. 45, my translation.)

If in our war-torn twentieth century we carry still the marks of this dual and conflicting conception of honor, we have likewise inherited a profounder philosophical analysis which aids me in coming to terms with our current perplexity of ending with honor. I refer to the philosopher

Hegel and to his attempt to overcome this duality of internal and external valuations of honor in his analysis of the master-slave struggle in history. Most of you will remember that this aspect of Hegel's thought was crucial for the young Marx in the formulation of his philosophy of history. But my purpose in summarizing it at the conclusion of this bare historical sketch of the concept of honor is to suggest its applicability to our reflections on the ending of wars in our time.

Hegel does not use the word *honor* but rather the word *Anerkennung*, which can be rendered imprecisely in English with words like *recognition, respect, acknowledgment.* His analysis of the master-slave struggle is not only historical, but also logical and ontological. The struggle for recognition or respect of one man for another or one group for another lies not only at the beginning of human civilization but also continues to take place in all forms of association at the family group, national, and international levels. Hegel calls it a life-and-death struggle because it involves the recognition of one's freedom or autonomy at the risk of one's biological existence. Man becomes truly man, no longer an animal, according to Hegel, when he is willing to risk his life in order to gain the recognition by others of his freedom.

The first outcome of this struggle is that one of the combatants submits to the other from fear for his life and becomes the bondsman or slave to the other who is master or lord. The master or lord has won the recognition for which he fought, and the slave, in fear for his physical life, is willing to acknowledge his lord and master and to serve him hand and foot. But in the course of time the master finds the enjoyment and leisure he has gained by his initial victory unsatisfying. To have his autonomy recognized by a servant is not sufficient. The servant, on the other hand, through the existential anxiety he experienced in the initial conquest, through serving his master, and above all through the subsequent work he is forced to do, gradually transforms himself and his environment. In the end he gains true freedom and recognition of himself as a builder and former of civilization, educating himself through fear and service and labor and transforming raw material products into human works, useful, practical, and artistic.

There is no need to enter into the complexities of Hegel's analysis, only to stress the results. The two great forces in human civilization, according to him, are fighting and working. As a result of the former, relations of dominance and submission are inevitably set up. Honor is demanded and given on the basis of inequality of external rank and position in society. However, war is not equal to constructive work and service in the long struggle for freedom as the mutual recognition of the equality of all men in respect to their essential humanity, that is, their inner freedom. Unlike his predecessor Immanuel Kant, Hegel believed that warfare is a necessary catalyst in building a civilization, but only a catalyst. The works of peace are those that produce genuine freedom as opposed to mere liberation. And the loser in a trial of warfare is likely to gain that true freedom in the end because he must undergo the disciplines of fear of death, service to others, and labor for suprapersonal goals. The fear of the Lord is the beginning of wisdom, Hegel remarks, borrowing from the Hebrew scriptures. Growth from that beginning comes in service to others, and work in building habitations for man on this earth brings the culmination of wisdom. If civilization begins in inequality and servitude, its goal is mutual recognition and respect of all by each.

If this brief excursus into the history of honor as a concept can teach us anything, it should remind us that honor pertains more properly to the ending of wars than to their beginnings. There was a time when this was not so. When wars resembled duels more closely, the point of honor lay in the occasion of the quarrel, not in its conclusion. Such is no longer the case. In focusing on the ending of wars, this Conference gives us opportunity to reflect on the present and possible future rather than on the past, on outcomes and consequences rather than on origins and causes. Accordingly, let me now turn to some thoughts on endings in my own lifetime.

When the soldiers of the Second World War returned to the United States, our welcome was a warm one, full of honor in both external and inner senses. We wore the symbol of the veteran, the so-called ruptured ducks, in our civilian lapels with great pride. They helped us to find our way back into normal society, into educational institutions, into jobs and professions, above all, into our home towns. The honors we warriors accepted were visible tokens of respect and recognition from a grateful populace. At the invisible level the honor we ourselves felt we had earned was even more important. In the life-and-death struggle we had emerged as masters, and our foes, Germany and Japan were our serfs or servants. Few of us pondered then how these honors were marred by the means we had employed to win, namely the terror bombing of civilians and our leaders' insistence on unconditional surrender of the enemy. Such means enabled us to enter their countries as conquerors and to observe their humiliation and total loss of rights, at least for the period before directives for ruling the defeated foe were hastily promulgated. There was something wholly primitive about this situation, akin to the Homeric wars at the beginning of Western civilization. Innocent and guilty alike were made to acknowledge their utter subservience. Ordinary German soldiers, many of whom had fought harder and longer than we, trudged homewards in decrepit uniforms to be greeted by hostile glances from their own townsmen, who were equally miserable and dishonored.

How different do these events appear in retrospect after twenty-eight years! By virtue of the anguish they suffered, by dint of hard and unremitting work—and, it must be added, by the generosity of the Marshall Plan—our dishonored foes have won in less than a generation the recognition that Hegel described at a philosophical level. Recently President Nixon was characterized in the press as being especially gratified to receive a visit from "Europe's cleanest statesman," Willy Brandt, holder of the Nobel Peace Prize! Such are the ironies of history.

We, their masters, have not fared so well. Our position today is more ambivalent than theirs. The American victory in World War II appears to have taught us the wrong lessons. It instilled in many Americans a great pride and dubious sense of superiority. As a consequence we have been hearing often of late the importance of being Number One in the world. The reference is always to power, to that political meaning of honor which Hobbes believed to be its only justified use. Whatever else we may think about this conception of honor, it is worth reminding ourselves that at the beginning of our national history honor was considered to be a much more inclusive concept.

Witness the closing words of the Declaration of Independence, by Thomas Jefferson: "And, for the support of this declaration, with a firm reliance on the protection of Divine Providence, we mutually pledge to each other our lives, our fortunes, and our sacred honor." Whatever connotation the word *honor* may have carried for the Founding Fathers, it is hardly an accident that the word appears last in this sentence and is alone qualified by the word sacred. Even allowing for rhetoric in such a revolutionary statement, it still seems worlds removed from the notion of honor derived from the latest reminders that we are the world's greatest military and economic power.

Unlike World War II, the Korean and Vietnam wars have not ended in military victory for the United States. For a people grown accustomed to the slogan "In war there is no substitute for victory," the ending of these last wars, particularly Vietnam, has appeared to be dishonorable. In our history there can have been few more poignant and painful contrasts than the welcome home we World War II veterans received and that accorded the Vietnam soldiers who did not become prisoners of war. Already overchallenged by the nature of that guerrilla conflict and demoralized by their experiences in Vietnam, millions of these youth have had to return to a society which regards their service to the country as either useless or mistaken, at worst nearly criminal. Their plight is a serious, often a desperate one, pregnant with tragic possibilities for our immediate future as a society. Sometimes they remind me of those straggling German soldiers at the end of the Second World War, to whom I gave a ride in my jeep on their way home.

The hard question we Americans must ask ourselves is whether peace with honor cannot be achieved in other ways than by unconditional surrender of our adversary. To those of us who conceive honor to be associated exclusively with power, with precedence, being Number One, the answer will be No. It will be too difficult for such Americans to accept the unwisdom of total triumph, particularly when the foe is of different ethnic origin than we. For such Americans it is simply intolerable that we lost so many soldiers in Vietnam in vain. They seemed to give their lives for nothing. Like the ancient Greek in Euripedes' play *Rhesus*, the survivors of Vietnam brood:

. . . 'Tis an evil doubly bad; to die with glory, if die one must, is bitterness enough . . . to him who dies; assuredly it is; though to the living it adds dignity and honor for their house. But we, like fools, have died a death of shame.

The spiritual consolation many parents and wives found in losing a family member in World War II appears to be denied to the present survivors of Vietnam. Instead there is in some a sense of shame, and shame is not only one of the most painful but also one of the most dangerous passions. Such a consideration has doubtless been partly responsible for our prolonging the war there beyond all rational considerations of a proper time for withdrawal.

To the failure to win a decisive victory must be added the widespread conviction that our cause in Vietnam was not a just one. In World War II few of us doubted for a moment that we were fighting for the right. In fact we Americans have long prided ourselves on winning our wars *because* we were virtuous. To be sure, such a persuasion is hardly unique to us as a people. But we seemed to have learned another wrong lesson from our triumph in the Second World War, where the moral sentiments of a large proportion of the world's peoples favored us, even our decision to demand unconditional surrender by our enemy. Thus our reversal of fortune in Vietnam, where we have not won and are unsure whether we deserved to win, is made doubly hard to bear. If we are really to have peace with honor there, a rethinking and reeducation of ourselves as a people appears to be the only remaining alternative.

It is here that I believe the Hegelian analysis has its contemporary relevance. That analysis suggests that the basis of all enduring honor among men and nations lies in a mutual recognition of each other as human beings, that is, as independent and autonomous. However diverse and manifold are the things that are honored from culture to culture and from one age to another, acknowledgment and respect for this aspect of our common humanity is surely the *sine qua non*. Furthermore, the possibility for such acknowledgment, respect, and recognition is to be rediscovered at the ending of wars rather than in their commencement or prosecution. Most of our wars have begun with the failure to accord to the foe just this recognition. As a war progresses, the bitterness induced by loss of life and cruel suffering makes that failure even more pronounced. It is true that an adversary who fights courageously and well against great odds calls forth in his opponents admiration and a grudging respect. In Vietnam, for example, many of our soldiers learned to esteem the fighting abilities of the North Vietnamese and Vietcong. Though courage in whatever form has always been closely associated with honor, and deservedly so, on the battlefield admiration for one's foe does not lessen the desire to kill him. And in every war I know of, there have been dishonorable acts enough to make suspect the claims to superior virtue of either side.

Only when hostilities have ceased is there real opportunity for the gaining of mutual respect in the ceaseless struggle of men for autonomy in inner and external forms. That opportunity lies in the work of reconstruction and reconciliation through work. As I see it, wars do not end honorably, but honor can accrue to the ending of them by virtue of the subsequent actions of both antagonists. When we begin to think what courage is, physical courage in warfare is likely to come first to our minds. But then we soon discover that civil courage is a more pervasive and enduring virtue, though difficult to define and rarer in appearance. It is hardly different with the sentiment of honor. Though the battlefield may be seen as a test of honor for individuals and groups, its real substance can only be established in the conduct of life in the occupations of peace.

A war that ends in a stalemate rather than a total victory for either side has greater potential, so I believe, for a longer peace to follow, if for no other reason than the chastening such an experience makes possible. In our century the peace that has followed wars has not lasted long, and the apparent victors at war's end have tended to become, in illustration of Hegelian dialectic, the vanquished. In good part a least this unhappy condition has been caused by the inability of the victors to discover the opportunities for growth beyond the ending. When the great powers, as they are called, interpret the glory they have supposedly won on the battlefield in terms of pride of place and power, there is no transition to the more difficult forms of honor appropriate to peace. It is just possible that a war like Vietnam that ends without victors may have better prospects in the years to follow. Since we know nothing about the future, pessimism is in any event as foolish as optimism.

But if prediction is futile, reflective attempts to understand the present situation can be very beneficial. In this Conference we are not dealing with the ending of war *per se*, but with the ending of wars. That choice of theme indicates to me at least that we have made an advance in understanding over our predecessors in earlier decades of this century. Perhaps there has been some gain in historical comprehension as a consequence of the calamities we survivors have endured.

What I have gained from surveying the concept of honor in its historical development and pondering its present usage in war and peace is a sense of its *necessary* duality of scope and meaning. On the one hand, honor is a sentiment internal to the individual, his conviction of self-worth and inner freedom. On the other hand, it is external to him in being dependent on his evaluation by others, a matter of his reputation. This double nature of the concept of honor has had a dialectical development in Western history. At times and among certain groups honor has signified the inner integrity of the individual alone and a corresponding indifference to external reputation. At other times, the reverse has been the case, and honor has been regarded as something bestowed by others in independence of inner sentiment. But it is crystal clear that man as a social being cannot live without both, however lasting the tension may be between inner and outer. When a society becomes politically tyrannical or when it disintegrates into mobocracy, the fruitful tension between honor understood as inner integrity and honor as external reputation disappears. In such societies the individual is forced either to retreat into himself or to become a tool of whatever power is momentarily dominant. A dynamic social structure, on the other hand, is one that holds both inner and outer conceptions of honor in fruitful interplay. The public person is not held to be merely an instrument of his constituents or superiors, and the private person is neither insensible nor indifferent to public affairs or reputation. Only then can honor become a promoter of social order and also a means to individual fulfillment.

In a war-wracked nation this double function of honor gets easily perverted. The inner and personal meanings become sundered from the social and political meanings, creating the confusion so common today about what honor really means. When a country becomes imbued with military conceptions of honor, it also narrows the range of the kinds of deeds considered honorable to those ascribed to someone by virtue of his rank and power in a hierarchy. Something of the same narrowing and perversion occurs in a thoroughly politicized society. If honor is something ascribed and bestowed, as is constantly emphasized in social science literature, it is no less true that it must be freely done by those who respect themselves. One does not freely honor a person unless he has some claim to excellence, in whatever field that excellence may lie. However diverse the achievements and qualities that have been honored in the course of history—and they have been very diverse indeed— worthiness of being honored has been a fairly constant prerequisite for full recognition.

This mutuality of recognition on the part of the bestower and the bearer of honor, as well as on the part of millions of spectators throughout the world, is the high stake in any lasting peace today. The profound and enduring sense of the master-slave analysis seems to be that survival is not enough. Men will forever risk their lives for the sake of the non-biological goal of respect or acknowledgment of their autonomy. In warfare they achieve this primordially human goal by force; in victory they compel respect from the defeated. But soon they discover that such compulsory respect is not truly satisfactory, does not really bring one to peace with himself. Recognition is something to be earned by the long and cooperative work of reconstruction of what has been gained or lost by violence. Only then, if at all, can honor regain both its inner-personal and external-social sense and significance. Political and military notions of honor are always subordinate to these personal and social meanings.

I began by commenting on the archaic and atavistic sound of the word *honor* in our time. The current confusion about its meaning I consider to be a consequence of our warring century, in which the military and political meanings have come to the fore. These incessant wars have weakened man's self-respect and consequently the respect he has for others, including international society. But if war is not to become the norm of national and international life, if we go to war in order to have peace, as Aristotle held, not the other way around, we shall have to regain the activating principles of honor as the freely accorded recognition of mutual worth and excellence. If we are to continue to believe that the ideal goal of our species is freedom for individuals as well as for nations, honor as a concept and reality can never be outmoded. For it serves to relate us, even to reconcile us under favorable conditions, to the actual world. There is no likelihood that the inner sense of integrity will ever be at one with social recognition and respect. But when the two are in creative movement and tension individually and collectively, we may at least hope for peace with honor.

DAVID LITTLE

8
THE "JUST WAR" DOCTRINE AND U.S. POLICY IN VIETNAM

It has never been difficult to show that arguments over the morality of U.S. intervention in Indochina have been conducted according to the categories of the so-called just-war tradition. The issues at the bottom of all such arguments have been whether the decision by the United States to use force in Indochina was (a) made on behalf of and in support of a legitimate authority; (b) based on just cause; (c) based on just intentions; (d) whether there was a reasonable probability for the success of the intervention; (e) whether the policy was proportional with respect to costs and benefits; and, finally, (f) whether it was sufficiently discriminate in relation to the lives and welfare of noncombatants.[1]

Similarly, the decisions according to which the United States ended its involvement in Indochina can be usefully discussed in relation to the same just-war categories. In fact, such a consideration illuminates old, as well as new, features that are relevant to a general moral evaluation of U.S. policy.

In undertaking our task, we must respond to the admonition that we "put Vietnam behind us," that all is over and done with there, and therefore retrospective reflection and evaluation serves no good end. The proper reply is that the "rights and wrongs" of U.S. policy are not yet completely settled, and sooner or later we shall have to think about those matters, simply because they are there. One hopes that can be done without vindictiveness and backbiting. But that hope imposes an important condition on the discussion. It need not preclude discussion altogether.

The appropriate focal point of U.S. disengagement from Indochina is the contents of the Paris Peace Agreements (January 27, 1973), as well as the context of intentions and expectations in which they were arranged, and the series of events subsequent to them which, at long last, produced "the final settlement." We shall therefore examine the content and context of the Paris Peace Agreements, and then the events subsequent to them, all in the light of just-war categories.

CONTENTS OF THE PEACE AGREEMENTS

It is interesting to recall that in honoring Henry Kissinger and Le Duc Tho on October 16, 1973, the Nobel Committee issued the following statement: "News of the Paris agreement brought a wave of joy and hope to the entire world. The . . . Committee hopes that the undersigning parties will feel *a moral responsibility* for seeing that the Paris agreements are followed" (italics added). The basis for "joy" and "hope," as well as for assuming "a moral responsibility" to implement the agreements, was, it would appear, the particular terms of the agreements. The major provisions seem to outline a just settlement, a settlement which, the Nobel Committee implied, ought, from a moral point of view, to be instituted.

1. In Article 9, the agreements recognize that "the South Vietnamese people's right to self-determination is sacred, inalienable, and shall be respected by all countries" (Ch. IV, Art. 9a), including, explicitly, the North Vietnamese (the DRV). Article 9 continues: "The South Vietnamese people shall decide themselves the political future of South Vietnam through genuinely free and democratic general elections under international supervision" (Art. 9b).

Moreover, Ch. V, Art. 15 reads: "The reunification of Vietnam shall be carried out step by step through peaceful means on the basis of discussions and agreements between North and South Vietnam, *without coercion or annexation by either party*, and without foreign interference" (italics added). In fact, in one place the agreements use the phrase "sovereignty of South Vietnam" (Ch. VI, Art. 18e). "Pending reunification," it continues, ". . . North and South Vietnam shall respect the Demilitarized Zone on either side of the Provisional Military Demarcation Line" (Art. 15b), recognizing that the DMZ is "not a [permanent] political or territorial boundary" (Art. 15a). Incidentally, the word *permanent* seems logically required in this context, since by the terms of

Art. 15b the DMZ is necessarily acknowledged as a *temporary* political dividing line, "pending reunification," as it states. Otherwise, Art. 15b would not make sense.

We ought to refer here to the curious matter of the continuing presence of DRV troops in the South. There is no direct reference in the agreements one way or the other to that presence—partly, of course, because the DRV never acknowledged their presence! But clearly the terms of Art. 15 support Kissinger's interpretation that "nothing in the agreement establishes the right of North Vietnam troops to be in the south." Indeed, any *use* of those troops, whether they be augmented or not, in coercing a settlement between the North and the South violates both Arts. 9 and 15.

2. Though the designation is anything but precise, the agreements recognize, and consequently extend political legitimacy to, "the two South Vietnamese parties," the Government of Vietnam (GVN) and the Provisional Revolutionary Government (PRG) (Ch. II, Art. 7 and Ch. IV, Art. 12). Art. 12 provides for the National Council of National Reconciliation and Concord, which is supposed to provide a framework for cooperation between the two parties, and to "organize the free and democratic general elections provided for in Art. 9b." While the agreements do extend limited legitimacy to the PRG, they leave the GVN intact, subject to the conditions of cooperating with the PRG and of observing the other conditions regarding cessation of hostilities (Ch. II), the return of captured military personnel (Ch. III), cooperation with the Joint Military Commission and the Commission of Control and Supervision (Ch. VI), etc.

3. Ch. VII, Art. 20a reads in part: "The parties participating in the Paris Conference on Vietnam undertake to refrain from using the territory of Cambodia and the territory of Laos to encroach on the sovereignty and security of one another and of other countries." Art. 20b continues: "Foreign countries shall put an end to all military activities in Cambodia and Laos, totally withdraw from and refrain from introducing into these two countries troops, military advisors and military personnel, armaments, munitions and war material."

4. Particularly Chs. I and II deal with the extensive restrictions on the United States and on "all other countries" regarding the direct use of force, or the introduction of more than "piece-for-piece" "periodic replacement of armaments, munitions and war material which have been destroyed," etc. (Ch. II, Art. 7).

These four items—the matter of North-South relations, of GVN-PRG relations within the South, of the relations between North Vietnam and surrounding countries, and of the relations of world powers to South Vietnam—establish a set of explicit and implicit understandings of relevance to consideration of several just-war categories.

Political Legitimacy in South Vietnam. There are two dimensions to the problem of political legitimacy in South Vietnam. In the first place, the agreements leave no doubt about the "sovereignty" or legitimacy of South Vietnam as an independent political entity. The agreements are in many ways built around the "right to Self-determination of the South Vietnamese people," a right that is asserted to be "sacred" and "inalienable."

The use of the words *sacred* and *inalienable* is important for our purposes. These "ultimate" words identify an overriding concern for and commitment to the freedom of South Vietnam from coercive interference. Moreover, they are more than "merely legal" words; they have a moral cast to them. Therefore, the agreements themselves, by using such language, invite analysis and reflection that transcends legal discussion; they beg for moral consideration, such as we shall try to supply.

Because of the moral implications of this language, a question is raised that is not expressly answered by the agreements: Ought the principle of self-determination be applied, as a moral matter, to South Vietnam in the way the agreements apply it? This has always been of course a hotly disputed question. My own view is that the emphasis in the agreements conforms to the deep and long-standing divergences between the northern and southern Vietnamese written about by so many scholars. Those deep divergences were reflected in Joseph Kraft's comment, a comment that has, to my mind, proved itself to be a kind of axiom in the discussion of the Indochina question: "In South Vietnam . . . there is a strong nationalist resistance. Millions of Buddhists, Catholics, refugees and ordinary workers and peasants abhor the North Vietnamese Communists."[2] (Incidentally, the popular contention that elections in South Vietnam in the mid-'50's would have produced overwhelming support for the North has finally been clarified and qualified in the Pentagon Papers.[3])

In the second place, it is important, if somewhat perplexing, that the agreements assign legitimacy directly to "the South Vietnamese people" as a whole, and leave ambiguous the legitimacy of "the two parties," the GVN and the PRG. Obviously, the ambiguity is a concession to necessity. No agreement on that issue could have been arrived at in Paris. Nevertheless, the phraseology is suggestive. Neither the GVN nor the PRG had, as a matter of fact, been able over time to command anything like total support from the South Vietnamese people, or to claim to be the exclusive representative of the aspirations of the South Vietnamese. Therefore, the question of legitimacy with regard to the "two parties" *has always been dependent upon a marginal, but highly important judgment between the two parties as to which one held out the greatest relative promise for expressing the independent aspirations of the South Vietnamese people.*

Though, admittedly, they do not make the point very precisely, the agreements appear to imply that governmental authority is contingent upon acting in a way that is in keeping with South Vietnamese independent aspirations (Ch. III, Art. 2a). Accordingly, governmental legitimacy is to be determined on the basis of a calculation of the relative probabilities for representing South Vietnamese self-determination. If what we suggested above is accurate, then this way of deciding upon political legitimacy in South Vietnam conforms to the reality of the situation.

Just Cause. Within the framework of the agreements, a just cause, or a justifiable reason for resorting to force, would exist if there were strong evidence of coercive violations of the central tenets of the agreements regarding North-South relations, GVN-PRG relations, DRV-surrounding country relations, and world power–South Vietnam relations.

Generally, the just-cause criterion, like the other criteria in the just-war tradition, is not self-applying. It calls for interpretation and judgment. It is especially important to ascertain the character, extent and purpose of the violations. In respect to the agreements, violations ought particularly to be judged by the degree to which they subvert the legitimacy of the South Vietnamese people, as described, not to mention the "sovereignty and security" of the Laotians and Cambodians. Extensive violations with respect to these matters are not the only potential causes for a justified resort to armed response, but they are central, given the language and the implications of the agreements.

THE POLICY CONTEXT OF THE PARIS AGREEMENTS

How did the agreements feature in the intentions, expectations, and plans—in short, in the respective policies—of the relevant parties: the United States, the DRV, the PRG, the USSR, the CPR, and the GVN? In the light of the subsequent debate regarding what the important signatories "really" expected to be the outcome of the Paris Agreements, this becomes an urgent, if complex, question. In any case, it leads us, in just-war terms, to a consideration of the intentions of the important signatories, and to the issue of whether those intentions were "just." That is, did the parties intend to act so as to avoid serious coercive violations of the agreements' provisions, and to help promote the objectives of the agreements?

The Intentions of the Important Signatories. To begin with, it is uncertain precisely what the United States intended to do about fulfilling the objectives, and what it expected that others intended to do about avoiding violations and achieving objectives.

On the one hand, the United States took the public position that the DRV had hitherto posed a serious threat to the sovereignty of the South Vietnamese people as well as of the Cambodians and Laotians, and that restraining the DRV was the *sine qua non* for achieving the objectives of the Paris Agreements. According to the U.S. position, there existed a new, realistic opportunity for restraining the DRV, thanks to a carefully developed military and diplomatic policy. The military side had consisted of "Vietnamization," the extension of armed conflict into Cambodia and Laos, and of selective applications of force like the "Christmas bombing" in December 1972.

The diplomatic side was built on détente with the USSR and China. Détente was above all the new context which was now to make possible the achievement of Paris objectives. For example, Kissinger was "pretty well convinced that [the United States] could achieve an 'understanding' with Russia and China to limit arms deliveries to [the DRV]."[4] Paris negotiator William Sullivan was even less tentative: "The North Vietnamese . . . will find it satisfactory, I think, to keep the agreements because there are external pressures which would lead it in that direction. It has discovered that the Chinese and the Soviets are not willing to go to the lengths that it would like them to go to commit themselves for its ambitions."[5] But columnist Chalmers Roberts summarized best of all the suggested link between détente and the feasibility of the central Paris objectives:

There are . . . two important differences between 1954 and 1973; the second Indochina War has taken massive tolls in men and wealth, and much of Indochina has been devastated. Even more important Hanoi's two principal allies, Moscow and Peking are in a new relationship now with Washington, one that would be endangered by a breach of the Paris Agreements.[6]

Consequently, Kissinger seemed confident that "the Communists were now committed to 'a political process,' meaning they had been forced to forsake military conquest in the foreseeable future."[7] In support of this Kissinger appeared to expect "the North Vietnamese troops in the south should, over a period of time be subject to considerable reduction . . ."[8] His comments regarding Laos and Cambodia were even more hopeful:

It is our firm expectation that within a short period of time there will be a formal cease-fire in Laos which, in turn, will lead to a withdrawal of all foreign forces from Laos and, of course, to the end of the use of Laos as a corridor of infiltration.

Secondly, the situation in Cambodia . . . is somewhat more complex . . . Therefore, we can say about Cambodia that a de facto cease-fire will come into being over a period of time relevant to the execution of the agreement.[9]

President Nixon, in public and private statements highlighted in the news, promised to use U.S. military power to enforce the basic objectives of the agreements, if they were violated by the DRV. But Kissinger's own language, just after the signing, made little use of threat. Instead, there was a broad tone of assurance, not only about U.S. resolve, but about the designs of the other side as well: "[I] t is our firm intention in our relationship to the DRV to move from hostility to normalization and from normalization to conciliation and cooperation. . . ."

All that is on one side. On the other, the United States leaves a quite contradictory impression regarding its own and others' intentions. It is an impression of fundamental indifference to the objectives of the agreements, aside from retrieving American POWs and disengaging itself from Indochina. And it is an impression of indifference to the designs of the DRV and its allies, designs that are perceived as antagonistic to the objectives of the agreements.

According to the revelations of Tad Szulc,[10] "the secret record shows that Kissinger told the Chinese premier that the trouble with the North Vietnamese was that they were too greedy, that they wanted everything at once, and that they were afraid of the process of history." Once the United States was out of Indochina, "history would run its own course in Vietnam" (!). Moreover, the "secret record," as well as the Kalbs's account, suggests that Kissinger was indifferent to the details of the agreements. He appeared simply to want a settlement that would extricate the United States from Indochina and thus eliminate an annoying impediment to the advancement of détente. In Szulc's words, Kissinger "seemed more interested in the technical modalities of the cease-fire provisions . . . and gave the impression that he had lost interest in the political fate of the rest of Indochina." Finally, though Kissinger talked confidently about a cease-fire in Cambodia and a "withdrawal of all foreign forces from Laos," this was not seriously expected.

As to the DRV's intentions regarding the objectives of the agreements, there is an ambiguity parallel to the ambiguity that is characteristic of U.S. intentions. On the one hand, the DRV consistently emphasized, prior to signing the agreements, respect for the self-determination of the South. The DRV meant only to aid the South in freeing itself of U.S. interference. Their argument, and that of many critics of U.S. policy, was that DRV action in Indochina has simply been "reactive"in response to illicit U.S. intervention. Once U.S. interference is removed, the South can freely determine its own future in relation to the DRV, as can the Cambodians and Laotians. The major objective is to permit a genuinely representative southern government to flourish, a government led, of course, by the PRG.

But, on the other hand, there is a different interpretation of DRV intentions, an interpretation more in line with Kissinger's assessment revealed in the "secret record." It is stated succinctly in Jean Lacouture's long-standing dictum: "Hanoi seeks to rebuild under its own rule or influence, the components of former French Indochina."[11] According to this interpretation, the DRV has never intended to cultivate a pluralistic political environment in Indochina. It has dominated the PRG from the beginning, and has always intended to extend that domination, regardless of the inclinations of the South Vietnamese people. In a somewhat less direct way, the same applies to DRV relations with Cambodia and Laos. Given such intentions with respect to South Vietnam, the PRG could never be expected, realistically, to express and implement the South's independent aspirations, for once the North had worked its will, those aspirations would necessarily be defined in terms of *northern* interests and objectives.

There have been divergent accounts of Soviet and Chinese intentions *vis-à-vis* the agreements. We have noted the optimistic U.S. view that they had perceived their interests to lie in helping to restrain Hanoi and thus to promote the objectives of the agreements. There are also accounts of indifference to those objectives, and of acquiescence in Hanoi's designs, once the United States had left, and so long as détente was not disturbed.

There are also reports of conflicting interests between the Soviets and the Chinese, and of tension between them as to who will wield greatest influence over Hanoi. But these differences occur within a framework of joint acceptance of the expansion of the power of the DRV in Indochina.

Finally, there is no ambiguity, either in the manifest or the secret record, that the GVN never intended to live up to certain aspects of the agreements. This was particularly true in the case of Art. 11, having to do with consultation and creation of a National Council of National Reconciliation and Concord together with the PRG, and in the case of Arts. 16, 17, and 18, having to do with the role of, and the responsibilities to, the Joint Military Commission and the International Commission of Control and Supervision (ICCS). GVN resistance to cooperation was, among other things, premised on the belief that the PRG was, in the last analysis, a stalking-horse for the DRV. Consequently, to the extent the PRG achieved power, the independent interests of the South Vietnamese people would suffer.

EVENTS SUBSEQUENT TO THE SIGNING OF THE AGREEMENTS

The events after January 27, 1973, that led up to total U.S. withdrawal from Indochina by April 30, 1975, are illuminating with respect to the three just-war issues we have touched on so far: the political legitimacy of the belligerents, the conditions that constitute a justifiable cause for a resort to force, and the character of the intentions of the relevant parties.

Because there is, in this subsequent period, evidence all round of violations of the Paris Agreements, it is necessary to balance and compare the violations on reaching a verdict on the question of who is morally entitled under the circumstances to resort to the use of force. In regard to the basic and clearly specified objective of promoting and protecting the "sacred and inalienable" right of the South Vietnamese people to self-determination, and of refraining from coercion against the South or against Cambodia or Laos, it now seems unquestionable that, compared with the activities of the GVN and the United States, the DRV committed the gravest violations, and, at least presumptively, gave cause for a responsive resort to force.

The pattern of flagrant violation was impartially documented but six months after signing. On July 21, 1973, the Canadian truce supervisory team, shortly before withdrawing from the ICCS in disgust, published a report harshly and extensively accusing North Vietnam of "massive" and "unrelenting" infiltration of troops into South Vietnam in deliberative violation of the Paris Agreements.

[The DRV] without being deterred one scintilla by the Paris agreement has been infiltrating massive armed North Vietnamese troop units into Cambodia and South Vietnam in order to conduct military operations against the Republic of Vietnam . . . . It can also be concluded that there never has been the slightest indication during the four and a half months following the cease-fire that the DRV has modified its infiltration policy.[12]

Against the background of the Spring 1975 invasion across the DMZ and other points, it is clear that the intentions of the DRV, as well as its allies, were never in the direction of military restraint and of dedication to "political competition" in the South. Moreover, and even more tellingly, there is not the slightest indication, since the victory of Northern forces, that an independent, broadly representative government will be allowed to develop in the South. According to latest reports, "although South Vietnam is nominally run by the PRG, it is becoming increasingly apparent that Hanoi makes the crucial decisions in the South and that the North Vietnamese are the real power in Saigon."[13] So much for promoting and protecting the "sovereignty of South Vietnam."

Indeed, the subjugation and enfeeblement of the PRG since the DRV's victory lends a certain retroactive credibility to the GVN's skepticism about dealing with the PRG. With all the deficiencies and disabilities of the GVN (to which we shall return), it now seems that *as between* the "two parties," the GVN "held out the greatest *relative* promise for expressing the independent aspirations of the South Vietnamese people," or at least of keeping options open in that direction. So far as I can see, all such options are now fast closing down.

It is not yet so clear how domineering the DRV will be in relation to the Cambodians and Laotians, nor whether the other neighboring countries in the area have good reason for the apprehensions they express in private. But in relation to Laos and Cambodia, there is no doubt that Ch. VII, Art. 20 was consistently disregarded by the DRV, and that the "sovereignty" of Cambodia and Laos will in the future be strongly conditioned by the interests and goals of the DRV.

If events in 1975 began to clarify the intentions of the DRV, and, to a lesser extent, those of Russia and China, regarding the objectives of the agreements, what of the intentions of the United States? Which of the two impressions was most accurate? Did the United States intend to support and promote the basic objectives of the agreements, and did it expect the DRV, together with Russia and China, to do so?

Despite the optimistic and confident impression given by U.S. officials, the underlying purpose of signing the agreements, it now seems obvious, was to enable the United States to disengage itself from Indochina, while at the same time retrieving the POWs. Furthermore, it is hard to believe that the United States expected the DRV to live up to the agreements. This conclusion is supported by the readiness of the United States to agree to the presence of 100,000 or so DRV troops in South Vietnam. That concession, which provoked Thieu's abiding wrath throughout the negotiations, was perhaps the crucial concession from the point of view of the DRV. It was, as Szulc says, "a veritable diplomatic bomb." It meant that the United States was prepared to withdraw all its military forces and yet leave the DRV in a forward position, a position from which it could continue to develop military pressure against the South whenever it so desired.

There was of course the reluctant promise of continuing U.S. military and economic aid to the GVN. But there was little else to inspire confidence that, beyond the extrication of the United States, the terms of the agreements mattered very much to the United States. This impression was reinforced by the congressional restraints that were imposed upon the use of U.S. force in that area. In short, even though, by the terms of the agreements, military response to DRV violations would seem to have been clearly warranted, the United States, both at the executive and the congressional levels, had precluded any reversion to the use of force.

The question therefore remains, was the U.S. policy of "permanent disengagement" in face of "massive" and "unrelenting" DRV violations of the agreements morally justified, according to just-war criteria? As I shall try to show, the answer is that permanent disengagement was morally justified, though like many moral decisions, the matter is slightly more complex than it seems.

EVALUATING THE POLICY OF "PERMANENT DISENGAGEMENT"

As I indicated at the outset, the just-war tradition provides several norms, rather than one, for evaluating the use, or the potential use, of force. Consequently, the various criteria, when applied to cases, must often be weighed against each other. Trade-offs must sometimes be struck. This was, I believe, the situation with respect to U.S. policy in the closing stages of its involvement in Indochina. The considerations of political legitimacy, just cause, and just intentions create, as I have argued, a *prima facie* case against the DRV and its allies, and therefore create a presumptive right in favor of a responsive use of force. But there are, as we must now hasten to note, countervailing moral considerations which ought, on balance, to have constrained the United States from acting on the basis of the right.

Reasonable Probability of Success. Given the assumptions of the agreements, "success" is defined in relation to achieving a situation in South Vietnam, Laos, and Cambodia where political decisions could be made that express "the independent aspirations" of the respective peoples, relatively free of external coercive interference. That objective has always implied two requirements: (1) restraining the DRV, and (2) creating a viable and reasonably representative government that could *in fact* express independent aspirations. The two requirements for achieving "success" have always been interrelated. The DRV's vigorous military activity in the whole Indochina area has unquestionably made the task of developing viable, independent governments more difficult. At the same time, in the light of the debacles in South Vietnam, Cambodia, and Laos in the spring of 1975 the failure to make any significant progress toward developing viable, reasonably representative governments compounded the difficulties of imposing military restraint on the DRV.

But these two requirements have been interrelated in still another way, a way that is more important from the point of view of U.S. policy. Insofar as the United States has intervened in the past to try to satisfy the first requirement—the military restraint of the DRV, it has in the very process *worked against* the second requirement—the cultivation of an independent, representative government. The story is familiar. By attempting to render South Vietnam (and Laos and Cambodia) independent of coercive interference from the DRV, the United States fostered in effect dependent, relatively unrepresentative regimes, regimes obviously too reliant for survival on continuing U.S. supervision and involvement. (I am assuming that the reasons for the GVN's collapse run much deeper than slackening U.S. aid, though that undoubtedly had an effect.)

In sum, the probability for the success (as defined) of renewed U.S. military intervention in face of serious violations of the agreements by the DRV was exceptionally low. The United States was caught in a massive contradiction of will. Doing the right thing (satisfying requirement number 1) meant doing the wrong thing (contravening requirement number 2). It may be true, as I believe it is, that the root cause of this contradictory predicament was the illicit intentions and actions of the DRV. But that does not change the difficulties of achieving success. To the extent that *ought* implies *can*, the United States was well advised to disregard under the circumstances an objective it could not achieve.

Proportionality: The Balance of Good over Evil Effects. If the central objectives of the agreements are one "good" that is, according to our argument, morally worthy of support and promotion, it is still necessary to "price" the achievement of those objectives, to weigh the overall costs against the benefits.

If, and so long as, it was possible to hold out some hope that the provisions of the agreements could be met, that the DRV might be restrained—perhaps by exhaustion, perhaps by the "changed attitudes" of the Chinese and the Russians—from mounting massive military intervention throughout Indochina, if, and so long as, the DRV might be expected to tolerate "political competition," then it seemed reasonable to accept a fairly high price in working to achieve the objectives of the agreements. However, after it became clear that the long-advocated "negotiated settlement" was an empty arrangement, the prospect of continuing substantial U.S. military involvement with no promise of genuine resolution seemed to demand too high a price in further destruction and loss of life. But the consideration of proportionality cuts still more deeply. The military policies that were in force just prior to the signing of the Paris Agreements (e.g., the "Christmas bombing"), were justified as being instrumental toward achieving "peace with honor." Specifically, Kissinger defended the December bombing of Hanoi as necessary in order to modify the intransigence of the DRV negotiating position. Because of the bombing, he suggested, the DRV changed its demands with respect to the National Council, agreed to "the specific identity of South Vietnam," and promised to respect the DMZ. If all these modifications had been translated into action, Kissinger's case would have been more plausible in terms of costs and benefits (overlooking, for the moment, the apparently indiscriminate character of the bombing raids). However, it is hard to see, after the North's conquest of the South a mere two years later, that the concessions were really "worth it."

Discrimination: Protecting Noncombatants. There has been much talk, since the Communist victories in Indochina, that the United States need not have lost the war if it had "done the job right." Had it employed force without all the restrictions regarding the protection of civilians, had it extended the pattern of the Christmas bombing to other areas or North Vietnam, possibly including the total destruction of the dikes, and so on, the outcome of the war could have been reversed. As an empirical matter, that is probably true.

But throughout the war, the U.S. government self-consciously excluded certain targets, weaponry, and military actions out of consideration for civilians. Though the U.S. military was selective in observing these restrictions, though it was unimaginative in minimizing civilian casualties and in easing the lot of the refugees, it did officially commit itself to the principle of discrimination. That is, in my judgment, the only defensible position to have taken, from a moral point of view.

But it follows from such a commitment that the United States is morally blameworthy for all deliberate or negligent indiscriminate acts (as were, of course, all other military forces in Indochina). The United States is also obligated to avoid all continuation or extension of such acts. Insofar as a renewal of U.S. military activity, after the breakdown of the agreements, would have "required," as was here and there argued, an extension of indiscriminate policies, such a renewal was morally excluded.

CONCLUSION

Our analysis, by means of some of the just-war categories, of the decisions leading to permanent U.S. disengagement from Indochina, indicates the *moral complexity* surrounding those decisions. While the determination "to get out and stay out" was, on balance, justifiable in terms of the overriding weight of criteria D, E, and F above, the results of our consideration of criteria A, B, and C introduced some strain and perplexity into the story.

One of the perversities of conveying an optimistic account of U.S. intentions and expectations regarding the feasibility of the Paris Agreements, as Kissinger, Nixon, and other officials did in early 1973, was to obscure this element of moral strain and contradiction in the momentous decisions that were being taken at that time. We were achieving, we were told, the "noble ideals" of political pluralism and self-determination in Indochina, and *at the same time* we were ending once and for all a costly, destructive intervention that had caused great agony from the very beginning. In fact, we were sacrificing the "noble ideals," undoubtedly for good reason, but we were doing it nevertheless.

That should have been made clear, along with the reasons why we were in the process of doing what we were doing. Not to make it clear, but instead to prattle—as President Nixon did—about "peace with honor," and solemnly to accept, as Kissinger did, the Nobel Peace Prize (Le Duc Tho, to his credit, refused), only served to deepen the cynicism in this country over political discourse, and of the possibility of speaking carefully and honestly about issues of such enormous moral significance as the termination of U.S. presence in Indochina.

NOTES

1. The various criteria of the just-war tradition differ in number from place to place. For simplicity and brevity, I have left out one criterion that is sometimes mentioned: that the initiation of armed conflict, as well as the conditions for settlement, must be duly and publicly announced.

2. Joseph Kraft, "The Administration's 'Cambodian Gambit,' " *Washington Post* (March 2, 1975).

3. *The Pentagon Papers*, The Senator Gravel Edition (Boston: Beacon Press, 1971), 4 vols, vol. 1, p. 246.

4. Marvin and Bernard Kalb, *Kissinger* (New York: Dell Publishing Co., 1975), p. 413.

5. William Sullivan, *Department Of State Bulletin* 68, 1756 (Feb. 19, 1973), p. 201.

6. Chalmers M. Roberts, "The Third Indochina War: A Question of Spirit," *Washington Post* (Jan. 25, 1973), p. A14.

7. Kalbs, *Kissinger*, p. 413.

8. Henry Kissinger, *Washington Post* (Jan. 25, 1973), p. A10.

9. Ibid.

10. Tad Szulc, "Vietnam: The Secret Record," *Washington Post* (June 2, 1974), pp. C1ff.

11. Jean Lacouture, "Uncle Ho Defies Uncle Sam," *New York Times Magazine* (March 28, 1965).

12. *Washington Post* (July 22, 1973), p. A1.

13. *Washington Post* (June 9, 1975), p. A16.

INDEX